ESSENTIALS

of Working Capital
Management

T0334438

ESSENTIALS SERIES

The Essentials Series was created for busy business advisory and corporate professionals. The books in this series were designed so that these busy professionals can quickly acquire knowledge and skills in core business areas.

Each book provides need-to-have fundamentals for professionals who must:

- Get up to speed quickly because they have been promoted to a new position or have broadened their responsibility scope.
- Manage a new functional area.
- Brush up on new developments in their area of responsibility.
- Add more value to their company or clients.

Other books in this series include:

Essentials of Accounts Payable, Mary S. Schaeffer
Essentials of Balanced Scorecard, Mohan Nair
Essentials of Business Ethics, Denis Collins
Essentials of Business Process Outsourcing, Thomas N. Duening and Rick L. Click
Essentials of Capacity Management, Reginald Tomas Yu-Lee
Essentials of Cash Flow, H. A. Schaeffer, Jr.
Essentials of Corporate and Capital Formation, David H. Fater
Essentials of Corporate Fraud, Tracy L. Coenen
Essentials of Corporate Governance, Sanjay Anand
Essentials of Corporate Performance Measurement, George T. Friedlob, Lydia L. F. Schleifer, and Franklin J. Plewa, Jr.
Essentials of Cost Management, Joe and Catherine Stenzel
Essentials of Credit, Collections, and Accounts Receivable, Mary S. Schaeffer
Essentials of CRM: A Guide to Customer Relationship Management, Bryan Bergeron
Essentials of Enterprise Compliance, Susan D. Conway and Mara E. Conway
Essentials of Financial Analysis, George T. Friedlob and Lydia L. F. Schleifer
Essentials of Financial Risk Management, Karen A. Horcher
Essentials of Foreign Exchange Trading, James Chen
Essentials of Knowledge Management, Bryan Bergeron
Essentials of Licensing Intellectual Property, Paul J. Lerner and Alexander I. Poltorak
Essentials of Managing Corporate Cash, Michèle Allman-Ward and James Sagner
Essentials of Managing Treasury, Karen A. Horcher
Essentials of Online Payment Security and Fraud Prevention, David Montague
Essentials of Patents, Andy Gibbs and Bob DeMatteis
Essentials of Payroll Management and Accounting, Steven M. Bragg
Essentials of Sarbanes-Oxley, Sanjay Anand
Essentials of Shared Services, Bryan Bergeron
Essentials of Supply Chain Management, Michael Hugos
Essentials of Technical Analysis for Financial Markets, James Chen
Essentials of Trademarks and Unfair Competition, Dana Shilling
Essentials of Venture Capital, Alexander Haislip
Essentials of XBRL, Bryan Bergeron

For more information on any of the above titles, please visit www.wiley.com.

ESSENTIALS
of Working Capital Management

James S. Sagner, PhD

WILEY

John Wiley & Sons, Inc.

For general information on our other products and services or for technical support, please contact our Customer Care Department within the United States at (800) 762-2974, outside the United States at (317) 572-3993 or fax (317) 572-4002.

Wiley also publishes its books in a variety of electronic formats. Some content that appears in print may not be available in electronic books. For more information about Wiley products, visit our web site at www.wiley.com.

Library of Congress Cataloging-in-Publication Data:

Sagner, James S.
    Essentials of working capital management/James S. Sagner.
        p. cm. — (Essentials series; 55)
    Includes index.
    ISBN 978-0-470-87998-6 (pbk.); ISBN 978-0-470-91690-2 (ebk);
ISBN 978-0-470-91691-9 (ebk); ISBN 978-0-470-91692-6 (ebk)
    1. Working capital. 2. Corporations—Finance. I. Title.
    HG4028.W65S24 2010
    658.15′244—dc22

                                                2010021353

Printed in the United States of America

10 9 8 7 6 5 4 3 2 1

Contents

Preface

This book is one of a series on essentials of finance. As the publisher observed the near chaotic conditions in the credit markets that began in 2008, it became apparent that there was a need for an explanation of business processes and specific ideas on changes to company structures and procedures.

Managers, regulators, and senior government officials have lived through the failure of Lehman Brothers and other organizations; the forced acquisitions of Merrill Lynch, Wachovia Bank, and many other firms; the decline in the Federal Reserve's benchmark lending rate to nearly zero; and the official U.S. unemployment hovering just below 10 percent. To survive, companies have been forced to make drastic changes in hiring, product development, expenses, and, of particular interest to our reader, in their management of working capital.

Working capital management is the art—and increasingly the science—of organizing a company's short-term resources to sustain ongoing activities, mobilize funds, and optimize liquidity. The most important elements are:

- The efficient utilization of current assets and current liabilities of a firm throughout each phase of the business operating cycle.

- The planning, monitoring, and management of the company's collections, disbursements, and bank account balances.

- The management of receivables, inventories, payables, and international transactions to minimize the investment in idle resources.

- The gathering and management of information to effectively use available funds and identify risk.

The liquidity crisis presently being experienced in the United States has been the subject of numerous articles, Congressional hearings, and general debate. Available data indicates that adjustments have been ongoing and may eventually lead to the opportunity for future business expansion once this period comes to an end. Despite some bankruptcies, companies have adjusted remarkably well to the contraction of credit and liquidity and to weakened economic conditions. Our discussion focuses on how businesspeople can continue to be successful in these difficult financial times, particularly in the context of limited access to bank credit and other sources of short-term funds.

Concept of the Book

Essentially, this book is a back-to-basics guide. In developing this approach, several components have been included to assist the reader.

- Chapters are of manageable length, typically less than 5,000 words.

- Each chapter contains brief sections of *Tips and Techniques* and *In the Real World*. *Tips and Techniques* are specific ideas to manage working capital in the context of the chapter topic. *In the Real World* includes explanations of how actual companies have implemented changes.

- Sections of a comprehensive working capital case—the Widget Manufacturing Company (Parts I, II, and III)—begin each major section. The purpose of this case is to demonstrate real-life situations that involve various management issues concerning current assets and liabilities. The questions at the end of the case are designed to generate thoughtful consideration of appropriate actions. Suggested solutions are included in Appendix A.

- Other useful material is contained in Appendices B, C, and D to supplement the coverage in the main part of the text.

In planning the content, the author and publisher had in mind the needs of several types of readers:

- New working capital managers, including students and recent appointees to any of the functions of working capital.
- Current managers who need a succinct, well-written reference.
- Members of allied professions, including accountants, information technology specialists, marketing and production managers, and others who want to expand their knowledge base.
- Readers outside of the United States who either plan to do business here or are observing their economy as evolving into a United States–type of capitalism.
- Senior managers who need an "executive summary" to understand working capital without becoming too enmeshed in detail.

Chapter Content

The layout of the chapters and supplemental material is described in this section.

Order of the Chapters

As previously noted, the beginning two-thirds of the book discusses concepts relating to significant working capital accounts. The last third focuses on the infrastructure of working capital—those activities that are essential for managers to proceed. Specific content is as follows: international working capital (Chapter 8), information and working capital (Chapter 9), and management of the working capital cycle (Chapter 10). For readers who want a quick recommendations summary, a list of ideas is in this final chapter.

Tips and Techniques and *In the Real World* examples are presented in every chapter. *Tips and Techniques* are suggestions to the reader regarding action steps to improve working capital. *In the Real World* examples are brief case situations from our experience in working with companies to improve working capital performance. At the end of the regular text content, we have included helpful appendices. As noted above, Appendix A contains a suggested solution for the comprehensive case, Widget Manufacturing I, II, and III; Appendix B covers basic capital structure concepts; Appendix C lists sources for additional information; and Appendix D is a glossary of important finance concepts.

Metrics

Ratio analysis and other metrics are used to provide a comparative basis for a hypothetical company versus its industry. We use plastics manufacturing as the industry comparison, although the reader should understand that each industry is unique. For example, companies that manufacture men's clothing experience a very long receivable cycle, often six months, while grocery stores and supermarkets are expected to pay their suppliers for certain food products in about one week.

Acknowledgments

The author is indebted to Michèle Allman-Ward, with whom he authored an earlier book in the Wiley Essentials series, *Essentials of Managing Corporate Cash* (2003), for her assistance in Chapter 8. Michèle is a distinguished consultant and lecturer and has an encyclopedic knowledge of global treasury management practices.

Chapter 9, Information and Working Capital, was coauthored with Arthur C. McAdams, a senior lecturer in the management department in the School of Business at the University of Bridgeport (CT). He was senior vice president and director of Information Systems at People's Bank (CT) leading the implementation of several strategic initiatives, and has many years of experience in systems development, project and process management, and business planning. Dr. McAdams has had articles published in leading technology journals.

Acknowledgment is also extended to Timothy Burgard, Helen Cho, and Laura Cherkas, my Wiley editors; and to my former colleagues and clients at First National Bank of Chicago (now JPMorgan Chase) and the team at Sagner/Marks.

You may have questions about the ideas presented in this book. If so, e-mail the principal author at jsagner@bridgeport.edu with your inquiries. However, a good place to start is to ask your bankers for ideas—often they are on the leading edge of current practice and have access to helpful product information.

CHAPTER 1

Concepts in Working Capital Management

After reading this chapter, you will be able to:

- Understand the concept of working capital.
- Appreciate the components used in managing working capital.
- Determine how ratio analysis is used in understanding working capital.
- Consider traditional and modern ideas of working capital management.

Working capital is the arithmetic difference between two balance-sheet-aggregated accounts: current assets and current liabilities. This calculation is done in a currency, such as U.S. dollars, which is the convention we will be using in this book.

Working Capital Concepts

Both current assets and current liabilities are comprised of several ledger accounts as shown *in italics* in Exhibit 1.1. For the company presented in this balance sheet—we'll call it the Rengas Company—the amount of working capital is $425,000, calculated as current assets ($650,000) less current liabilities ($225,000).

EXHIBIT 1.1

Rengas Company Balance Sheet
(As of December 31, 2010)

Assets		Liabilities and Owners' Equity	
Current assets	*$65,000,000*	*Current liabilities*	*$22,500,000*
Cash	*5,000,000*	*Accounts payable*	*15,000,000*
Short-term investments	*15,000,000*	*Notes payable*	*6,000,000*
Accounts receivable	*27,500,000*	*Accrued expenses*	*1,500,000*
Inventory	*15,000,000*		
Prepaid expenses	*2,500,000*	Long-term liabilities	40,000,000
		Bonds payable	20,000,000
Fixed assets	60,000,000	Mortgage payable	20,000,000
Plant and equipment (at cost)	100,000,000		
Less: Depreciation	(40,000,000)	Owners' equity	62,500,000
		Common stock (50,000 shares)	10,000,000
		Retained earnings	52,500,000
Total assets	$125,000,000	Total liabilities and net worth	$125,000,000

Description of Working Capital Accounts

The accounts noted in italics are briefly explained below, with chapters of this book devoted to appropriate management procedures.

- *Cash accounts and short-term investments.* These account categories include cash on hand and in bank accounts, and any short-term investments that are expected to be turned into cash within one year. We'll review the management of cash in Chapters 2 and 3, and of banking relationships in Chapter 4.

- *Accounts receivable.* This category of current assets includes all credit sales where the customer is expected to pay by a future date specified on an invoice. Most companies have small amounts of uncollectible credit sales, and an account called "allowance for doubtful accounts" may be deducted from accounts receivable to reflect this experience. We'll examine receivables in Chapter 5.

- *Inventory.* Most companies hold some combination of raw materials, work in process (that is, partially manufactured and assembled), and finished goods. There are various accounting practices for valuing inventory and management concepts regarding inventory, which will be discussed in Chapter 6.

- *Payables.* The accounts payable account represents the amounts owed to creditors for purchases. Payroll is the other significant component of payables. Issues regarding payables will be reviewed in Chapter 7.

- *Other working capital accounts.* Prepaid expenses and accrued expenses often appear on balance sheets. Prepaid expenses are assets paid in advance of expenses as incurred. For example, insurance is paid in advance of the incurrence of the expense. Accrued expenses are costs that have been incurred as of the date of a balance sheet but not paid. An example is payroll for employees whose expenses have been incurred but not yet paid.

There are numerous considerations in the optimal management of working capital. For example, what are appropriate procedures to manage cash? To reduce accounts receivable? To improve the performance of accounts payable? We will examine these and many other issues throughout this book.

Ideas Basic to Working Capital

Various concepts and conventions are used to explain and illustrate ideas on working capital management.

- The term *bank* refers to commercial banks, although other financial services companies and some vendors provide many of the services described. Vendors are noted when the relevant topic is discussed; for example, payroll services are provided by four leading firms that are noted in Chapter 7. Freight invoice auditing firms are also discussed in that chapter, but there are so many companies in that business that we have not attempted to list them.

- Float is critical to an understanding of working capital. The concept of *float* refers to funds in the process of collection or disbursement. While the complete elimination of float is impossible, the calculation of the amount of float is critical in considering alternative processes. For example, in Chapter 2 we will examine the bank product of *lockboxing*. In deciding on the use of this service, we need to know the potential to save collection float as compared to the current system.

- Concepts that are basic to finance but not defined as working capital are reviewed in Appendix B. These include fixed assets, long-term liabilities and owners' equity on the balance sheet, and relevant income statement accounts. In addition, we demonstrate the calculation of the *cost of capital* (also called *weighted average cost of capital* or WACC), which is used to value float. The WACC is the weighted average of a firm's cost of debt (after tax) and cost of equity (common stock and retained earnings), and is expressed as a percentage.

- Opportunity audits should be conducted by relevant functions to analyze each element of working capital. For example, in payables, managers examine the percentage of payments made by check, the cost of those transactions, the extent of cash discounts offered and taken, the results of account reconciliation, the incidence of fraud, and other issues. As an essential part of this process, it is useful to document the delays and organizational units involved in the movement of forms, files, and other records including computer systems; see *Tips and Techniques: How to Be a Working Capital Consultant.*

How to Be a Working Capital Consultant

The traditional functional scheme of corporate management—such as sales, manufacturing, finance, and technology—prevents any one manager from having direct responsibility for working capital. Most often the only common manager is the chief executive officer (CEO) or chief operating officer (COO), who seldom has knowledge of or interest in the specific functioning of those activities. In order to better understand and analyze working capital flows, here are the suggested steps in a process often referred to as an *opportunity audit.*

❶ Prepare a "payment stream matrix" listing the working capital flows by name, dollar volume, and manager. The matrix becomes a road map to understanding and improving the business by indicating those major activities that drive short- and intermediate-term successes and failures. A working capital flow is an activity of the organization that generates a cash inflow or outflow. Inflows, or collection flows, are often products or services; outflows, or disbursement flows, are accounts payable (to vendors for purchases), payroll, and other uses of cash.

❷ Use the matrix to bring other disciplines within your organization into your working capital review. It is usually necessary to involve managers in all of the functional areas of the business, including sales, operations, and finances. Input from customers and vendors can be helpful in understanding how a transaction occurs from their perspective, and to make the process more efficient and effective for all parties.

❸ Focus on the major flows—usually those that have $1 to 2 million per month in activity—to allow you to develop improvements through the application of technology, redesign of existing processes, and consideration of outsourcing to banks

TIPS AND TECHNIQUES (CONTINUED)

and vendors. Consider both float (valued at the cost of capital) and processing expenses to build a baseline of costs, and then consider various new approaches to find efficiencies.

- Once opportunities for improvement are identified and solutions evaluated, senior management should be consulted for permission to proceed. See *Tips and Techniques: How to Overcome Resistance to Change* for ideas on coping with internal resistance.

TIPS AND TECHNIQUES

How to Overcome Resistance to Change

Bringing change to companies is often an extremely difficult task regardless of the logic of an innovation or the demonstrable savings that will result. Here are some ideas on meeting internal resistance.

- Solicit the support of senior management. Promote the program through presentations to middle managers and educational events to explain where opportunities can be found.

- Reward employees who work outside of finance for each idea suggested and accepted, and then again when it is successfully implemented. These incentives really draw company employees into the change process and foster an environment that controls naysayers.

- Use any available marketing devices to publicize the effort, including articles in the company newspaper, announcements at company meetings, e-mails messages, and promotions through cafeteria or lunchroom events. If your company can sell a product or service, it can sell working capital efficiency!

Ratio Analysis

The various accounts on financial statements (the balance sheet and the income statement) can be used to provide critical information about a company to financial managers, bankers, investors, and other interested parties. Ratio analysis allows us to quickly examine a company's financial statements to determine how performance has changed over time and/or how it compares with its competitors.

How Ratios Are Constructed

Data are entered into a numerator and a denominator and then divided to allow the calculation of a relationship that is considered meaningful. We can compare these data to previous years to see if a company's financial position is improving or deteriorating; this is called *longitudinal analysis*. We can also compare a company to others in the industry in the same time frame; this is known as *cross-sectional analysis*.

Finding truly comparable companies is difficult because no two organizations are exactly alike. They may have different geographic coverage, varying product lines, significantly dissimilar economies of scale, or other distinguishing characteristics. We'll attempt to compare actual companies in their industry while noting these discrepancies later in this chapter.

There are three sets of ratios in general use: (1) liquidity, (2) activity utilization, and (3) profitability. We'll review the ratios that specifically impact working capital using Exhibit 1.1 data as supplemented by the income statement data shown in Exhibit 1.2.

Working Capital Ratios

The important working capital ratios are noted below. Examples of other ratios will be noted in later chapters. We'll call the fictional business used for this chapter's ratios and throughout this book the Rengas Company.

EXHIBIT 1.2

Rengas Company Income Statement (For the Year Ending December 31, 2010)

Sales	$150,000,000
Less: Cost of goods sold	(100,000,000)
Gross profits	50,000,000
Less: Selling and administrative expense	(20,000,000)
Less: Depreciation expense	(5,000,000)
Operating profit	25,000,000
Less: Interest expense	(4,000,000)
Earnings before taxes	21,000,000
Less: Corporate taxes (at 35%)	(7,350,000)
Net income after taxes	$13,650,000

Liquidity

Liquidity refers to a company's cash position and its ability to pay its bills as they come due. The phrase "cash position" is not limited to cash on hand and in the bank; it includes access to bank loans and short-term investments as well. Liquidity should not be confused with profitability or net worth; a company could earn accounting income with significant assets, and yet go bankrupt for lack of working capital.

The two liquidity ratios are the current ratio and the quick (or acid test) ratio.

- The *current ratio* is calculated as follows:

  current assets ÷ current liabilities

  From Exhibit 1.1, the result is 2.9 ($65,000,000 ÷ $22,500,000).

- The *quick ratio* is considered more useful because it eliminates inventory in the numerator, on the theory that this asset could be stale, worn, or not saleable except at bargain prices. The quick ratio is calculated as follows:

$$(\text{current assets} - \text{inventory}) \div \text{current liabilities}$$

or 2.2 ([\$65,000,000 − \$15,000,000] ÷ \$22,500,000).

There are no standard ratios that solely measure cash (as a current asset) or cash flow (cash receipts − cash disbursements). However, *Troy's Almanac* (cited in the section "How Ratios Are Used") calculates total receipts (revenues from all sources) to cash flow, and cost of goods sold to cash flow. We will discuss this further in Chapter 10.

Activity Utilization

The *activity utilization* ratios indicate how efficiently the business is using its assets. The important working capital utilization ratios are receivables turnover (and its complement, average collection period) and inventory turnover (and its complement, inventory turnover days).

- *Receivables turnover* is calculated as follows:

$$\text{credit sales} \div \text{accounts receivable}[1]$$

  For simplicity in this discussion, we'll assume that there are no cash sales, with the receivables turnover determined as \$150,000,000 ÷ \$27,500,000, or 5.5 times.

- *Average collection period* is calculated as follows:

$$\text{receivables} \div \text{daily credit sales}$$

  In this example, we'd divide \$27,500,000 by (\$150,000,000 ÷ 360), with the result of 66 days.

- *Inventory turnover* is calculated as follows:

$$\text{cost of goods sold} \div \text{inventory}$$

  or \$100,000,000 ÷ \$15,000,000, which is 6.7 times.

---

1. Only credit sales are used because any cash sales would be collected immediately; therefore no receivable would be created. The term *receivables* refers to accounts receivable.

- *Inventory turnover days* are calculated as follows:

  360 days ÷ inventory turnover

  In this example, we'd divide 360 ÷ 6.7, which is 54 days.

Profitability

Although *profitability* is not an explicit component of working capital, it is included here because any change to working capital components directly impacts profits. In fact, if profit ratios have deteriorated or are below those of competitors, this may indicate working capital improvement opportunities. Important profitability ratios are profits to sales (ROS) and return on equity (ROE). The term "return" is another word for profits, and these ratios calculate the after-tax returns.

- *Profits to sales* (sometimes called "return on sales" or ROS) is calculated as follows:

  profits after taxes ÷ sales

  or $13,650,000 ÷ $150,000,000, or 9.1 percent

- *Return on equity* (ROE) is calculated as follows:

  profits after taxes ÷ owners' equity

  or $13,650,000 ÷ $62,500,000, or 21.8 percent

- There are a few industries where the ROE is considered of secondary importance to the ratio that measures the return on assets (ROA). For example, this ratio is widely used in banking to determine the profitability of a bank based on its asset base. The calculation of *return on assets* is as follows:

  profits after taxes ÷ total assets

  or $13,650,000 ÷ $125,000,000, or 10.9 percent

Leverage ratios are discussed separately as there are no direct working capital issues; see *In the Real World: The Other Category of Ratios: Leverage*. However, leverage indirectly affects working capital because of the impact on required cash payments for interest or the expected cash payments for dividends.

The Other Category of Ratios: Leverage

There is a fourth important category of ratios—financial leverage—that measures the extent to which a company uses debt as a source of its capital. The *financial leverage* ratio is calculated as follows:

total debt ÷ total assets

Another important leverage ratio, *times interest earned,* measures the number of times that income covers the obligation of paying interest on debt. This ratio is calculated as follows:

income before fixed charges (including lease payments and interest) and taxes ÷ the total of fixed charges

We do not include these ratios in a working capital discussion because the components do not appear in the current portion of the balance sheet.

How Ratios Are Used

We cannot use these ratios without reference to either earlier results, say from 2008 and 2009, or to those from competitive companies. The issue of finding reasonable "comparables" is made possible through industry ratios published by such sources as *RMA Annual Statement Studies* (published by the Risk Management Association); and Leo Troy, *Almanac of Business and Industrial Financial Ratios* (published by CCH [Commerce Clearing House]).[2] Selected ratios are also at *Value Line* (published by Value Line Inc.); Standard and Poor's Industry Surveys (www.standardandpoors.com/products–services/netadvantage); Dun

---

2. These three sources are available in the business reference sections of many libraries. See Appendix B for a listing of useful references and web sites. Troy can also be located at www.books.google.com/books?id=5nEsDHfsfFworking capital&dq=leo+troy%2Bcash+flow&source=gbs_navlinks_s.

& Bradstreet (www.dnb.com); and financial web sites like www
.hoovers.com.

The main difficulty in using these sources is that each business has its
own marketing processes, market coverage, and product lines, and when
aggregated into an industry, company uniqueness loses meaning. That
problem aside, we can compare the calculated current ratio of 2.9:1
(read as "2.9 to 1") to the industry's result. The general rule when using
industry comparisons is that any result within the interquartile range is
considered normal, and that any result outside of that range is unusual
and worthy of further analysis.[3]

In our situation, 2.9:1 can be too low compared to the industry,
which is unlikely, or too high, which is quite possible. In other words,
there may be an efficiency problem when ratios are too high, usually
indicating that too much of a numerator (such as an asset or a group of
assets) are being used to support a denominator (such as a liability or a
group of liabilities). It may be a more serious problem when there is too
little of a numerator supporting a denominator, as this could indicate a
possible future liquidity, activity utilization, or profitability crisis.

Significance of Working Capital

Why is working capital management important? In truth, businesses
have not paid sufficient attention to working capital in previous years,
and have focused instead on such concerns as raising and using debt and
equity capital, choosing information and manufacturing technology to
run operations, and attempting to develop domestic and global marketing strategies to sell product. However, recent economic problems have
forced companies to consider ways to improve profitability, cut costs,
and make business processes efficient. These are not just necessary
actions—they are required for survival!

---

3. The *interquartile range* refers to the area in an array of results from the twenty-fifth to the seventy-fifth
percentiles (or the first to the third quartiles). An *array* is a listing of the members of a group in either
ascending or descending order. The middle item in an array is the *median* (the fiftieth percentile), while
the *mean* is the arithmetic average of the total of all items divided by the number of items.

Working Capital: Traditional View

Working capital traditionally has been considered as a positive component of the balance sheet. That is, good performance for the current ratio has been considered as a result well in excess of 1:1, with the higher the numerator, the better; similar results hold for the other working capital ratios. For example, $3 million of current assets compared to $1 million of current liabilities is a current ratio of 3:1, or a three times "cover."

This thinking has been driven by the attitude of lenders and financial analysts that working capital constitutes a store of value for repaying such debts as borrowings. Bankers are trained to look at financial ratios and demand numbers that exceed preset standards. Often this demand is to enable the bank to force a company to borrow to put more cash on the balance sheet, thereby growing the bank's loan portfolio.

Working Capital: Modern View

The newer view is that working capital is undesirable because it constitutes a drag on financial performance. Current assets that do not contribute to ROE hinder the performance of the company, and hide obsolete inventory that may not be saleable, receivables that may not be collectible, and other problems. The emphasis is now on reducing current asset accounts to the point that current liabilities can be funded from the ongoing operations of the business. That is, cash collected from sales is used to pay for payables and payroll, with the minimum in idle current asset accounts.

The concept of working capital as a hindrance to financial performance is a complete change in attitude from earlier conventional wisdom. However, working capital has never actually contributed to a company's profits or losses; instead, it sits on the balance sheet awaiting disposition. No profits are directly generated by cash or accounts receivable, and inventories provide returns only when sold at prices above cost. In fact, there is a significant cost in carrying working capital, which can be calculated using the cost of capital; see Appendix B.

If the financial manager attempts to drive working capital down to nearly zero, he or she must actively manage each asset and liability category. Today, the discipline of working capital management is a growing field of practice that involves financial managers, marketing managers, accounts receivable and payable managers, order-entry and invoicing supervisors, and other staff. See *In the Real World: Dell's Management of Working Capital* for a discussion of one company's approach to working capital.

IN THE REAL WORLD

Dell's Management of Working Capital

The twenty-first-century approach to working capital management has been effectively implemented by Dell Computer and several other companies. Dell accepts ownership of components shortly before the start of manufacturing, driving raw materials inventory to minimal levels. Products are sold and a collection transaction is concurrently initiated, using credit cards or payments through electronic mechanisms, eliminating most accounts receivable. Dell manages the operating working capital or *cash conversion cycle* (CCC) to attain a zero net time for days of sales inventory minus days of payables outstanding.

The CCC is defined as the number of days between disbursing cash and collecting cash in connection with undertaking a discrete unit of operations.

$$= \frac{\text{Inventory Conversion Period}}{} + \frac{\text{Receivables Conversion Period}}{} - \frac{\text{Payables Conversion Period}}{}$$

$$= \frac{\text{Average Inventory}}{\text{Cost of Goods Sold}/365} + \frac{\text{Average Accounts Receivable}}{\text{Revenue}/365} - \frac{\text{Average Accounts Payable}}{\text{Cost of Goods Sold}/365}$$

Dell has actually attained a quarterly cash conversion cycle of *minus* eight days!

Managing working capital to nearly eliminate current assets and liabilities requires that cash not be expended to prepay for inventory or other operating costs, that vendors hold title to goods until delivery is requested, and that redundant expenses be eliminated where possible. A considerable inventory position is warehoused by cooperating vendors within minutes of delivery to a Dell factory, and is requisitioned once a customer sale is booked. Since some suppliers are reluctant to do business with these requirements, Dell buys from fewer than fifty companies, down by 75 percent from a decade earlier. Another innovation is the direct shipment of video displays to customers by the vendor based on an e-commerce instruction from Dell. This saves the cost of a second shipment, worth $30 per display.

As the result of these various actions, Dell's inventory turnover (for the year ending in January 2009) was an astonishing 57.8 times versus a median 6.3 times for the computer manufacturing industry, and its receivables turnover is 9.5 versus a median 8.0 for the industry. How does working capital affect Dell's financial statements? In the most recent reporting period, Dell's ROE was 58.0 percent, while the industry was earning 16.1 percent. And over the five-year period prior to the credit crisis that began in 2008, the ROE of Dell was 63.1 percent versus the industry's 32.2 percent.

Applying These Ideas to a Real Business

Thus far we've been considering a fictional company's financials. Now we'll look at the working capital results for Best Buy (stock ticker symbol BBY), a leading consumer electronics retailer operating over a thousand stores primarily in the United States. Best Buy's business strategy centers on meeting individual consumer electronics needs with end-to-end solutions, which involves greater employee involvement and increased services.

What Is Best Buy's Industry?

We noted earlier the problem in defining the industry from which to develop ratios for purposes of comparing equivalent companies, those in similar lines of business. Most observers would agree that Best Buy had a direct (although smaller and far less successful) competitor in Circuit City, but that company ceased operations in 2008. Others competing with Best Buy include Game Stop and Radio Shack. When searching for an industry, we could use "radio, television, and other electronics stores" from *RMA Annual Statement Studies*, but there are certainly other industry classifications that might be acceptable.

Whatever the industry, these retailers are experiencing severe price competition from discounters like Wal-Mart, direct mail sellers like Amazon, and warehouse stores like Costco. There have been various responses to this development, including the closing of marginal operations and the layoff of employees, more aggressive management of operations through leaner inventory and other actions, and the expansion into more profitable foreign markets like Asia (particularly China) and Canada. As an example of this last trend, Best Buy now does about one-fifth of its business in other countries.

Working Capital at Best Buy

The achievements of Best Buy can be traced to the retailing "category killer" concept,[4] which involves megastores with the size and general appearance of warehouses. These operations have an enormous assortment of merchandise, low prices, and self-service that is supported by staff trained in specific electronics product lines. Successful retailers have been able to seize market share from smaller operators who do not have

---

4. Examples of category-killer retailers include Wal-Mart (discounting); Home Depot and Lowe's Companies (building supplies); Bed, Bath and Beyond (home furnishings); Staples and Office Depot (office supplies); AutoZone (auto parts); and TJX Companies, the Gap, and Limited Brands (apparel). Although the category killer is not generally applied to companies that are in other industries, a few equivalent examples might include Apple (computer hardware); Goldman Sachs, T. Rowe Price, and PNC Financial (financial services); Coca-Cola, Colgate-Palmolive, and PepsiCo (consumer nondurables); and Celgene, Gilead Sciences, and Teva Pharmaceuticals (biotechnology).

the buying power to negotiate vendor discounts on inventory or the cash reserves to advertise aggressively or train staff. The consumer knows that prices are consistently low, so there is little reason to wait for special sales or to comparison shop.

Companies operating category killers have discovered that a key to this retail model is inventory, ordering process, transportation, and warehousing. The process is highly automated in modern distribution centers through the use of bar-coding equipment to scan and direct merchandise to holding bins or directly for delivery to stores. As inventory is sold, computerized information notifies distribution to begin replenishment and marketing to match sales to projections. We see this in the ratios in Exhibit 1.3, with inventory turnover at 7.2 turns versus the industry median of 6.6.

The other working capital ratios indicate similarly superior performance compared to the industry median. Furthermore, Best Buy managers understand that the capture of a market is a strategic process and cannot be accomplished in one quarter (the interval when public company earnings are reported). The compound growth rate for Best

EXHIBIT 1.3

Best Buy and Industry Working Capital Ratios

	Best Buy (BBY)	Industry		
		First Quartile	Median	Third Quartile
Current ratio (to 1)	1.0	1.1	1.3	1.9
Quick ratio (to 1)	0.4	0.2	0.6	1.2
Receivables turnover (turns per year)	22.9	8.5	19.6	40.0
Inventory turnover (turns per year)	7.2	4.0	6.6	11.7
Return-on-equity (%)	22.0	4.4	17.4	30.4

Source: RMA, *Annual Statement Studies* (2008–2009), and BBY Corporate Reports (2009).

Buy over the past 10 years prior to the current economic crisis was 16.5 percent, while competitors experienced flat or negative growth.

In terms of operating revenues, Best Buy now has three-fourths of the volume reported by the industry,[5] versus just over one-third 10 years earlier. It is likely that the current recession will continue to weaken competitors, perhaps forcing them to terminate operations (such as Circuit City) or close stores, while Best Buy has substantial liquidity and can withstand slower consumer traffic. By 2012, Best Buy could easily have 80 to 85 percent of the industry's volume.

Summary

Working capital involves two balance-sheet-aggregated accounts: current assets and current liabilities. The performance of these accounts is measured using ratios to examine a company's financial statements, allowing the determination of how performance has changed over time and/or against competitors. The ratios in general use calculate (1) liquidity, (2) activity utilization, and (3) profitability as compared to such standard sources as *RMA Annual Statement Studies* and *Troy's Almanac*.

Working capital was traditionally viewed as a positive component in managing a business; the modern view is that it constitutes a drag on financial performance. Current assets that do not contribute to return on equity hinder the performance of the company, and may hide obsolete inventory that may not be saleable and receivables that may not be collectible. The focus is now on reducing working capital accounts to the point that current obligations can be funded from the ongoing operations of a business.

---

5. Using the definition of the industry used by Standard & Poor's in its *Industry Surveys: Specialty Retailing—Computers and Electronics*. Within all of specialty retailing, only Home Depot (at $71.3 billion) and Staples (at $23.1 billion) are of roughly similar size to Best Buy (at $45.0 billion).

PART I

Cash—Transactions, Banking and Credit, and Financial Instruments

*N**ote:* This is the beginning of Widget Manufacturing Case—Part I. Parts II and III of the case open Parts II and III of the book. A suggested solution is provided in Appendix A. As noted in the Preface, the purpose of the case is to present a real-life situation that involves various issues concerning the management of working capital.

Comprehensive Case: Widget Manufacturing Case I

It was beautiful and sunny just before the Memorial Day holiday when Arnold Parks left a difficult meeting with his banker, Uriah R. Clueless (U. R.) of Second National Bank of Chicago. Arnold and his father, Arnold Sr., who had established Widget Manufacturing, have banked with Second Chicago for almost 30 years. U. R. had just informed Arnold that the bank would not extend their line of credit beyond the current amount. In addition, the overdue portion of notes payable must be paid within three months—by Labor Day. Although Arnold was irritated by this young lender's demand, the note was over 30 days past due, and Arnold did not see how any more than a token payment could be made during the next 60 days.

Widget was founded in 1946 by Arnold's father shortly after he had completed his military service in World War II. The company originally focused on radio components and eventually branched out into various types of consumer electronics products. The current product line supplements nationally advertised merchandise in many stores using the retailer's own private brand, offering a cheaper price to consumers than name brands. Shortly after 1950, the first salesmen were hired to call on stores in the Midwest. During the next decade, the business continued to grow, and by 1976, when Arnold took over as president, annual sales had risen to $75 million.

Cash Cycle

Although some stray checks (about 10 percent of the total billed) are received in the Chicago headquarters, Widget's manufacturing facilities are individually responsible for their own billing and collections activities. Customers are instructed to mail their remittances to the address of the plant responsible for the merchandise; the plants are located in the following cities:

Televisions and radios	St. Louis, MO
Wireless telephones and related equipment	Decatur, IL
Laptop computers and related equipment	South Haven, MI

The mail is delivered by U.S. Postal System local route mailmen to each of the plants between 11:00 AM and 2:00 PM daily.

On the first business day of the month, the plant manager at each location reviews the prior month's ending balance at the local bank and determines if cash is above or below the target balance level. He or she deposits excess cash to the concentration bank (Second National) by mailing a check drawn on the local bank, or draws down cash to cover shortfalls by depositing a concentration bank check at the local bank. The plant managers also prepare forecasts of cash requirements for the current month. They fax their month-end cash positions, transfers by check, and cash forecasts to the corporate treasurer, Bernie Paydoff, by the second business day of the month.

Bernie gets daily balance reports on his computer from the concentration bank, which has a target balance of $1 million in the master account, and estimates his cash position by 1:00 PM. When there is excess cash, it is invested in overnight repos in increments of $50,000. Shortfalls are covered by borrowing against a revolving line of credit at the concentration bank for which the company is currently charged prime + 3 percent (although this is likely to increase the next time credit is negotiated).

Bank Relationships

A monthly cash forecast is compiled, and Bernie reviews the balances and transfers cash to or from the corporate concentration bank to maintain the local account target balances that he has established. Bernie does not monitor the local bank balances because they are usually stable during the month once all the plant managers have made their deposits and withdrawals (discussed in Part II). If one of the business units requires an emergency infusion of cash during the month, the plant manager calls Bernie to report that he or she is writing a check against the concentration account. As long as there is an adequate amount in the account, Bernie does not worry about funding it until the normal month-end cycle.

Widget maintains relationships with several banks around the country, primarily because of the decentralized nature of the organization, the autonomy granted to plant managers, and the concern for access to borrowing should Second Chicago pull its credit line. Though none of the business units negotiates individual credit facilities with its banks, each maintains its own noncredit services. The plants and the home office maintain a general operating account at a local bank. This account is used for deposit of all remittances and payment of all expenses, except payroll. Payroll accounts are maintained at separate banks, primarily because each of the plant managers wants to deal with more than one local bank.

In the past, Arnold had only dealt with his high school friend, golfing buddy, and banker Ira M. Cash (I. M.), and after talking about their favorite rounds of golf and their 12th-grade antics, an increase in the line of credit had always been granted without I. M., even after looking at the financial results. However, today's meeting had been depressing.

Three months ago, I. M. had been promoted to a senior vice presidency in the bank and Arnold had been introduced to U. R. Clueless, who had asked to see an up-to-date set of financial statements at their first meeting. After reviewing these reports (see Exhibit I.1 to Exhibit I.3), U. R. talked about cash problems and even noted the possibility of a financial emergency. There had been no backslapping, no reminiscing about the time they tied the vice principal to the flagpole, and no golf stories.

Questions to Consider

Question 1. Calculate the most important financial ratios and compare Widget's results with industry averages. What do these ratios indicate?

Question 2. What changes do you recommend to the cash cycle of the Widget Company?

EXHIBIT I.1

Significant Industry Ratios

	Industry Average
Current ratio	2.75
Quick ratio	1.63
Receivables turnover	7.72
Average collection period (in days)	47.48
Asset turnover	1.96
Inventory turnover	7.02
Return on equity (%)	25.95

EXHIBIT I.2

Income Statement (in $ millions)

	Widget $	Widget %
Net sales	$931.6	100.0%
Cost of goods	(683.9)	(73.4)
Gross profit	247.7	26.6
General and administrative expenses	(179.1)	(19.2)
Depreciation expense	(16.8)	(1.8)
Interest expense	(30.2)	(3.2)
Earnings before taxes	21.6	2.3
Income taxes	(7.3)	(0.8)
Net income	**$14.3**	**1.5%**

EXHIBIT I.3

Balance Sheet (in $ millions) (% to Total Assets and to Total Liabilities and Equity)

	Widget $	Widget %
Cash	$ 8.0	0.97%
Inventories	285.2	34.14
Accounts receivable	217.8	26.07
Total current assets	511.0	61.18
Net fixed assets	324.3	38.82
Total assets	835.3	100.00
Accounts payable	98.2	11.76
Notes payable	112.1	13.42
Other current liabilities	8.6	1.03
Total current liabilities	218.9	26.21
Long-term debt	289.3	34.63
Total liabilities	508.2	60.84
Stockholders' equity	327.1	39.16
Total liabilities and equity	$835.3	100.00%

CHAPTER 2

Cash: Management and Fraud Prevention

After reading this chapter, you will be able to:

- Understand the significant components of cash.
- Appreciate the bank products useful in managing paper and electronic forms of cash.
- Determine how to reduce float and processing costs associated with cash.
- Consider various techniques of managing the risk of theft and fraud that affects cash.

*C*ash includes any generally accepted form of payment, including coins, currency, checks, and the electronic mechanisms of Federal Wire Transfer (Fedwire) and Automated Clearing House (ACH). In this chapter, we focus on these cash transaction forms, as they are the most widely used in business. The use of cash to complete business transactions is the obvious essential element in operating any company. We expect to be paid in cash or its equivalent when we sell our goods and services, and we know our employees and vendors will only accept similar methods of compensation when we pay our bills.

Forms of Cash

There are three forms of cash, each of which has to be proactively managed to attain the optimal working capital position.

1. Bank cash, including cash in the process of collection or disbursement (referred to as *float* in Chapter 1).

2. Cash to which access has been arranged through a bank line of credit, accessible whenever a shortfall of cash from operations is forecast.

3. Cash invested in short-term investments in order to earn a return, but which can be quickly turned into actual cash through the liquidation (sale) of the asset.

The management of each of these forms of cash constitutes a separate set of procedures and skills, and an overreliance on any one form may significantly increase the cost associated with cash and/or the risk of not having adequate liquidity to pay bills when they are due. In this chapter, we emphasize bank cash and float. In Chapter 3, we discuss the other forms of cash. See *In the Real World: Real-Life Collection and Disbursement Failures* for examples of companies that were *reactive* in managing cash; that is, they permitted long-established routines to continue and ignored appropriate financial practices.

IN THE REAL WORLD

Real-Life Collection and Disbursement Failures

Situation I: A company received checks in the mail, created a deposit ticket, and had one of the employees walk the deposit to the bank on her way to lunch. The bank was located in an office plaza adjacent to the company's offices. This activity occurred every day at about the same time, so passersby could watch her on her journey. One of these observers realized that the employee was fairly defenseless, so he grabbed her bag containing the deposit, knocking her down and injuring her in the process, and easily got away. The deposit, which included checks and some cash, was never recovered.

Situation II: Checks for monthly retail services were sent to a company whose name included the word "the" (as in "The Wiley Group"). The checks were received in the mailroom, which opened all mail and directed it to the appropriate area of the organization. All checks were supposed to be sent to the finance group to be copied and then deposited. One of the mailroom clerks noticed that some company names in the "pay to the order of" line left a space between the words "the" and the company's name. When that occurred, the clerk inserted an O or an A in a matching ink to change the recipient name to Theo or Thea, then stole the check and deposited it in a bank account he had opened in that name (as in Theo Wiley Group). Months passed before customers realized that they had never received credit for their payments and notified the company.

Situation III: An insurance company issued a check for $70 to settle a claim for property damaged by their policyholder in an auto accident. The check was altered to $7,000 using inexpensive desktop technology and cashed. Three months passed before the fraud was discovered and by that time the check recipient had disappeared.

Each of these situations resulted from sticking to accepted routines, the failure to consider risk, and a lack of knowledge of modern cash management procedures. Situations I and II could have been avoided through the use of lockboxing; situation III could have been prevented through controlled disbursement. We examine those products later in this chapter.

Essential Cash Management Elements

As noted in Chapter 1, the two critical factors in the optimization of cash are float and processing expenses.

1. An understanding of float is critical because all elements in the timeline of collections and disbursements have inherent delays, and

delays cost your company. Although we cannot eliminate float, we can examine every step of the cash-flow timeline to search for savings opportunities.

2. Processing expenses are similarly important as each transaction—whether performed internally or outsourced—has a cost, and that cost directly impacts your profitability.

Both factors can be managed through the use of various bank and vendor products.[1] In *Tips and Techniques: Collection Float—Base Case*, we examine a company's float and processing costs. Later we'll analyze changes that make operating procedures more efficient.

TIPS AND TECHNIQUES

Collection Float — Base Case

Here is a simple illustration of how float and processing expenses occur in a transaction cycle and the opportunities for savings. You use a bank to deposit your cash receipts—assume $200,000 per day in 500 payments (including checks and other forms of collection) from the sale of products and associated revenues. We'll look at each component of the collection cycle later; for now just consider those checks you received at your office in the regular mail delivery at 11:30 AM.

As the USPS mailperson is leaving, your office staff heads off to lunch, not to return until 12:30 PM. The mail is then distributed and opened, checks are pulled and copied, and your treasury manager prepares a deposit ticket. It is now 1:30 PM. The office assistant drives the deposit to your bank located in a shopping center perhaps two miles away.

What are the costs so far or are yet to be incurred? The answer may surprise you but is critical in understanding your working

1. For complete information on bank products, including features and costs, contact your banker. For the names of reputable commercial banks, see Appendix C or contact the national organization for cash and treasury management, the Association of Financial Professionals, at www.afponline.org.

capital opportunities; we review each delay and processing expense in this chapter.

❶ Time in the mail from your customer to you (mail float): 3.5 days.

❷ Time lost before your deposit begins to be processed by your bank (holdover float): 1.0 days.

❸ Time to convert your deposit to "good" funds (availability float): 1.5 days.

❹ Total staff time to prepare and make the deposit: 3.5 hours.

What happens next is the application of receipts to accounts receivable, resolving any discrepancies, and the verification of the stamped deposit ticket copy against the bank's deposit report. We must decide what to do with the "good" funds we receive— invest, reduce existing loans, or pay incoming invoices or payroll. Finally, we must pay the bank for its services.

❶ Time to apply receipts to receivables and verify the deposit: 3.5 hours.

❷ Time to manage "good funds": 1.0 hour.

❸ Bank fees to handle deposit and report on the daily transaction: $0.25 per check, $2 per deposit, and $1 per daily report.

This all adds to a surprising amount of annual cost.

Baseline

Float:	6 days @ $200,000 per day and a 10% cost of capital = $120,000
Staff time:	1 day @ $200 × 250 business days = $50,000
Bank charges:	$125 × 250 business days = $31,250
Total:	$120,000 (float) + $50,000 (staff time) + $31,250 (bank fees) = more than $200,000!

Note: The $200,000 is based on a $50 million-per-year business working 250 business days a year. All staff hourly costs are valued at $25 including benefits.

While we cannot eliminate the $200,000, we can manage this amount down to a somewhat smaller cost.

Lockboxing

The United States is a nation of check writers; although the volume has fallen from the peak of about 55 billion checks several years ago, some 30 billion are written every year by companies, individuals, and governments.[2] The origin of our use of so many checks—which is very different from other countries—goes back to our national banking system, which prohibited interstate banking from 1927 (the McFadden Act) until the mid-1990s (the Riegle-Neal Act of 1994, fully implemented in 1997). During those seven decades, banks were generally restricted to performing transactional activities in their states (and in some states like Illinois, the counties in which they were domiciled).

Interstate transactions involve a time-consuming check-clearing process, with the Federal Reserve and private clearinghouses exchanging physical checks from the bank of first deposit to the drawee bank (the bank on which the check was drawn). Many companies continue to use regular depository accounts for any checks received in their offices; this is inefficient (due to float considerations) and potentially risky (due to the possibility of theft). Various products have been developed to efficiently manage these paper transactions, the two most important of which are lockboxing and controlled disbursement. Traditional bank products have significant disadvantages; for an explanation, see *In the Real World: Why Regular Checking Accounts Should Be Avoided.*

IN THE REAL WORLD

Why Regular Checking Accounts Should Be Avoided

Companies often use regular checking (depository) accounts at their banks. This practice should not be followed because of various cost and fraud problems that may result.

---

2. See "The 2007 Federal Reserve Payments Study," at www.frbservices.org/files/communications/pdf/research/ 2007_payments_study.pdf. The Federal Reserve conducts payment surveys every three years.

- *Control of access.* Regular bank accounts are difficult to monitor in terms of access, as companies often allow several authorized check signers to disburse deposited funds. The purpose of such payments may be entirely legitimate, but controls are often weaker than on lockbox and controlled disbursement accounts managed by the treasury staff, and internal auditors may only review the bank statements every two or three years. Furthermore, a disgruntled former employee who has taken check stock may write those checks to a phony business, and then pocket the funds.

- *Multipurpose accounts.* Bank accounts are frequently opened at each facility of your organization for the convenience of staff, check encashment (cashing employee checks), or other reasons. Large companies with widely separated operations may receive requests to have access to local banks. If funds are collected by a branch, the office manager may simply open a local account, deposit these receipts, and disperse the funds for local expenses. All bank account activity should require a Board of Directors' resolution, and any violations should be treated as a serious breach of company policy.

- *Concentration of funds.* In Chapter 4, we examine concentration banking, the movement of funds from depository accounts to your major banking relationship. It is perhaps sufficient to note here that multiple bank accounts require time-consuming, active management with associated processing costs, or you could choose to leave the funds in the depositories, which will cost you float.

- *Too many accounts.* As merger activity resumes, the surviving company may find that the number of its bank accounts is excessive and expensive. However, it may be reluctant to close accounts against which checks may have been written or which receive deposits. It is difficult to manage a large account configuration, particularly as accounts may have different purposes, authorized signatories, and other characteristics. Some accounts may be dormant, yet are costing you monthly bank fees. Investigate the entire banking system and close accounts wherever possible.

Lockboxing Procedures

Lockboxing is a service that comprises several elements:

- Customers directly mail remittances to a bank-controlled post office box in major cities.

- Banks pick up mail numerous times each day beginning early in the morning.

- Mail is delivered to the bank's processing site.

- The lockbox area opens the mail, pulling out checks and remittance advices.

- The lockbox personnel determine if any checks should not be deposited based on instructions from the company (such as the wrong payee or a post-dated payment, one dated later than the current date).

- A copy or image of each check is created.

- Acceptable checks are encoded[3] and deposited.

- Availability is assigned, showing how rapidly the checks will be considered as collected funds based on the drawee bank, the bank on which the check is drawn.

- Summary information is sent to the company about the remittances, followed by electronic or paper versions of remittance documents and copies of the checks.

Lockboxing relieves companies of the burden and delay of handling mail and check deposits. The original form of lockbox services—known as wholesale lockbox—was established to handle low-volume, high-dollar checks. Critical data fields are manually key entered from the remittance document such as the customer and/or invoice number. A retail lockbox is based on automated processing of scan lines (known as

---

3. *Encoding* is the process of entering the dollar amount of the check on the bottom of the face of the check.

magnetic character ink recognition, or MICR, lines) of documents and is used primarily for consumer payments.

Imaging is a technology that permits the digitized scanning, sorting, cataloging, and retrieval of paper documents, including checks, remittances, envelopes, and correspondence. The manipulation of an image replaces the labor-intensive process of handling wholesale lockbox items, while increasing the flexibility of the data captured and the scope and speed of receivables information transmitted to the company.

How Does Lockboxing Reduce Float?

Lockboxing eliminates the delays experienced when checks are directed to a business. The sources of these delays include:

- *Late delivery of mail to suburban locations.* Mail may be one-half to more than one day slower arriving at a noncentral city location, say on Tuesday at noon instead of Monday at 10 AM, because of additional sorts and longer routes to reach the final destination.

- *Holdover of mail due to internal processing steps.* As an example, one company had a 24-hour turnaround rule, meaning that mail had to be processed and moved along within a day. The problem was that there were four separate workstations and four days before the checks were deposited!

- *Depositing of checks at suburban banks.* For convenience, many companies use nearby branches of their banks for deposits. The problem is that the bank courier stops by once a day at each branch, often as early as noon. Missing the courier's pick-up means a one-day delay in starting the check-clearing process.

- *Check clearing. Availability float* is the term banks use to assign "good" or collected funds to checks that are deposited. Availability is based on a bank's recent experience in clearing the checks it receives, and is measured in zero days (for Treasury and on-us checks),[4] one day (for major city and nearby suburban checks), two days (for distant locations), and three or more days (for checks written on nonbank financial institutions and foreign checks). Locating your depository distant from where checks are drawn can increase availability float by one-half day or more.

Lockbox speeds all of these activities, and can result in a savings of up to one-half of current total collection time, which can be six or more days. Refer to the *Tips and Techniques* boxes in this chapter for the calculation of the cost of float. Costs vary depending on the services provided by the bank, but it is never more than about $1 per transaction for wholesale lockbox and $0.50 for retail lockbox.

How Does Lockboxing Prevent Fraud?

Fraud may occur when cash and accounting functions are performed by the same individuals in a business office. Lockboxing places all cash handling under the management of a bank, which takes full responsibility for opening mail, pulling checks and other documents received, and making deposits of monies received. Notification is sent to client companies by various media as to each day's activity. Any loss due to bank error or theft is the responsibility of that financial institution.

In this situation, the only checks that are not under the direct supervision of the bank are those that are mailed or couriered to an office address rather than to the lockbox, and those handed to sales representatives rather than mailed. If a company aggressively prevents these practices, the possibility of theft is largely eliminated.

Controlled Disbursement

Controlled disbursement became a viable product in the early 1980s when the Federal Reserve System began to provide banks with early morning information on check clearings to be made that day. Like

---

4. *On-us* checks are written on and deposited into the same bank.

lockboxing, the product offers both float and control features that are superior to regular checking. In a regular disbursement account, checks can be presented until the time of the bank's closing, usually 4 PM. This requires that idle cash balances be maintained in those accounts to cover such checks.

Controlled Disbursement Procedures

Controlled disbursement accounts are located at large banks in suburban or rural locations specifically established for the purpose of receiving the presentment of a cash letter once or twice daily in the early morning hours.[5] The bank notifies its corporate customers by mid-morning of that day's checks clearing (or debiting) against the account. The customer then funds the debit once daily, eliminating the need to leave balances awaiting possible later clearings. Banks offering this product hold any checks received later in the day or make clearing adjustments the next day for debiting to the account, therefore eliminating the need for supplemental funds transfers to cover any shortfall.

Funding options include an internal bank transfer, an electronic transfer through Fedwire or ACH, both of which are discussed in the next section. The ACH credit does not become good funds until the next business day. Therefore the bank will require the equivalent of the average check clearings of one or more days to be maintained in the account to cover the ACH float. Controlled disbursement costs about $0.10 to $0.15 per item.

Account Reconciliation

Any disbursement account must be reconciled monthly to match the bank's records with the company's own books and so that neither party

---

5. The Fed actually delivers a *cash letter* (or grouping) of clearing checks to a bank operation in a noncity location (known as a Regional Check Processing Center [RCPC], or a country point). Recent changes in check processing allow the electronic delivery to these banks of check images, which will significantly speed the processing. This was accomplished through the Check Clearing for the Twenty-First Century Act (or Check 21), which took effect in 2004, and allowed the recipient of a check to create a digital version of the original check, eliminating the need for further handling of the physical document.

has made an error that goes uncorrected. Banks now provide automated partial or full reconciliation to the company within 5 to 10 days of the month-end. *Partial reconciliation* is simply a list of paid or cleared items, including information such as check numbers and dollar amounts that the company must then reconcile against its own ledgers. The cost is about $0.03 per item.

An affiliated (and recommended) bank product is full reconciliation, which takes the issued and cleared item files and matches them monthly. Companies are notified of matches, outstanding checks, items cleared but not issued (when the bank did not receive the issued file or notice of a late exception item), duplicate items ("forced postings"), and other problems. This step can assure that only checks properly issued are charged against the account. Full reconciliation costs about $0.05 per item.

How Does Controlled Disbursement Improve Float?

Controlled disbursement can improve float by extending the clearing time required for a check to travel from the deposit bank back to the drawee bank. This occurs because the drawee bank is located outside of major cities where clearing times are expedited by access to transportation, and because there are only one or two morning presentments of cash letters. The extension of float is typically about three-fourths to one full day. Assuming a company issues $100,000 a day in vendor payments (excluding payroll), the gain is about $10,000 a year in float (at a 10 percent cost of capital).

How Does Controlled Disbursement Prevent Fraud?

Controlled disbursement contains no fraud prevention controls, but associated products do allow financial managers to discover suspect checks. Many companies support controlled disbursement with *positive pay*, which requires that a file be sent to the bank containing the number and amount of each check issued that day. As the issued checks clear, the bank matches the number and amount to the check issued file. If any mismatches occur to either factor, the bank asks the company for accept or reject decisions. The daily files of issued check information can be accumulated by the bank into a file for monthly account reconciliation purposes.

Assuming that the protocols are followed, the honoring of any fraudulent check is prevented, such as those resulting from alteration (e.g., $70 was changed to $7,000 in *In the Real World: Real-Life Collection and Disbursement Failures*) or counterfeiting (e.g., the entire check is phony, which may result from using manipulated check images). Some banks now offer payee positive pay, which matches the payee's name on clearing checks to the issued file along with the check number and amount. Positive pay costs about $0.05 per item.

Bank Products Used for Electronic Transactions

There are two electronic bank products in wide usage for business-to-business transactions: Fedwire and ACH. We are not including credit and debit cards, ATM (automated teller machine), or value-added cards in this discussion, as they are used almost entirely for business-to-consumer transactions.

Federal Wire Transfer

Federal wire transfer (Fedwire) is processed on a same-day basis without settlement risk to the participant, as the Federal Reserve System guarantees payment. Fedwire is used infrequently by most companies, because there are few situations where funds must be moved that day. Financial services companies are the largest users of this system due to the volume of the funds and their value, and because regulations governing these industries force the immediate crediting of funds to investors' accounts.

Fedwire advantages are the following:

- *Value.* Immediate, same-day value.

- *Speed.* Very fast, although a few hours' delay may occur at peak operating times.

- *Security.* Reliable and secure.

Disadvantages are the following:

- *Cost.* Expensive to use relative to other payment types; at about $15 at each end of the transaction, or $30 or more, Fedwire is 200 times the cost of ACH.

- *Limited automation linkages.* Not all financial institutions are online with the Fed and so have to make alternative arrangements, which can slow the process and introduce errors.

Automated Clearing House

ACH networks offer an electronic alternative to checks.[6] The ACH system was established to effect inexpensive settlement of low-value, high-volume, and repetitive payments on an electronic, batch, overnight basis. Credit transactions are used for direct deposits of payroll, pension, and annuity payments. Debits transactions, also known as direct debits, are used for consumer bill payments, such as utility bills, phone bills, and insurance premiums. Corporate use has been largely for cash concentration[7] and payroll. The total number of ACH transactions is now about 15 billion a year, about one-half of the number of checks written.

ACH advantages include the following:

- *Value.* Payments can be made on precise settlement dates.

- *Reliability and efficiency.* Compared with checks, ACH collections follow a more predictable pattern.

---

6. There are various ACH rules governing payment formats; the interested reader should refer to the web site of the Electronic Payments Association at www.nacha.org.

7. *Cash concentration* is the accumulation of collected funds in checking accounts into a central account for purposes of investing or funding disbursements. This topic will be discussed in Chapter 4.

- *Electronic processing and interfaces.* ACH allows for automated interfaces to reconciliation and cash application systems.

- *Payment options.* ACH handles debit as well as credit transactions, providing opportunities for improved collection processes.

- *Information.* Large amounts of information can be transferred with the payment.

- *Cost.* The typical ACH charge is $0.15 (or less for high volumes).

ACH disadvantages include the following:

- *Delayed settlement.* ACH payments settle the day following the payment's initiation; in contrast, Fedwire settles same day.

- *Finality.* ACH does not offer the same guarantee of finality as Fedwire, as debits can be returned unpaid.

Terminal-Based Electronic Payments

Banks have long provided access to Fedwire transfers for their business customers through terminal-based electronic systems; we'll discuss information products in Chapter 9. Fedwire transactions have various levels of approval, requiring that separate, designated financial managers set up, sign off on, and release any disbursements; in this way, fraud can occur only through the collusion of several individuals. Companies can now send and receive ACH transactions through the Internet with equivalent safeguards. *Tips and Techniques: Collection Float—Improvements* discusses attempts at developing operational efficiencies.

Why Do Frauds Still Occur?

We have spent some time in this chapter discussing ways to prevent fraud. Despite the proven efficacy of bank products, frauds do occur to the extent of some $5 billion a year in the United States.[8] Common reasons are noted after the Tips and Techniques box.

---

8. This statistic is for check frauds and is attributed to the U.S. Secret Service; other sources at least double that estimate. See www.stopcheckfraud.com/statistics.html.

Collection Float—Improvements

Do you remember our earlier collection costs of about $200,000? Based on the ideas discussed in this chapter, the float time can be reduced to 3.5 days and the staff time can be managed down to 3.5 hours. The float reductions are in mail, holdover, and availability float, as discussed earlier in the chapter. The staff time is in the processing of mail, creating the bank deposit, and in taking the deposit to the bank. The bank charges will rise by the lockbox cost, which will include an incremental $75 per month for the product and $0.75 per lockbox deposit.

First Scenario

Revised float:	3.5 days @ $200,000 per day and a 10% cost of capital = $70,000
Revised staff time:	3.5 hours @ $25 per hour × 250 business days = $21,875
Revised bank charges:	$31,250 (deposits and other charges); $75 per month × 12 months; $0.75 per lockbox item × 500 items × 250 business days = $93,750
Revised total:	$70,000 (float) + $21,875 (staff time) + $93,750 (bank fees) = $185,625

A good start—we just saved $15,000 annually. Now let's try a little harder. This alternative assumes that we can convert one-fourth of our mailed payments to the ACH.

Second Scenario

Revised float 2:	The float will continue for the 75% of the items that are checks, or $52,500; for the 25% that are converted to electronic, the float is one day or $50,000 calculated at a 10% cost of capital = $57,500

Revised staff time 2:	No change from first revised staff time = $21,875
Revised bank charges 2:	$31,250 charges continues; the lockbox costs are 75% of the first revision or $46,875; the electronic receipts typically cost about $0.25 each, or $12,500 = $90,625
Revised total 2:	$57,500 (float) + $21,875 (staff time) + $90,625 (bank fees) = $170,000

Now we're saving $30,000 a year. And we have other benefits that we did not have earlier:

- Control—all payments are directed to a lockbox or are paid electronically, so no cash is touched by your employees.

- Convenience—the bank handles tasks that can require several hours each day of employee time.

- Credit and collection information—you know the same day whether your customers have paid their invoices and if it is appropriate to ship them new merchandise.

The true savings are certainly greater than $30,000, because you have avoided theft, saved employee time, and learned as soon as possible whether you've been paid. Each company must determine the value of these savings, but $50,000 a year (on an original cost of $200,000) is certainly within the experience of U.S. companies.

- "We're too small": Companies below about $500 million in annual sales have a higher rate of fraud than large businesses do. Smaller companies often do not separate accounting and cash handling responsibilities, and this situation is an invitation to employee fraud and should be avoided. This is a particular problem with long-term, trusted employees who are "above suspicion" of larceny or other criminal behavior.

- "Our bank doesn't have these products": Bankers may not call on smaller companies to explain cash management products, either because potential revenues are too small or because the banker does not understand or does not have the product. The solution is for the financial manager to become educated about these products and contact community and/or regional banks that can provide them.

- "Our auditors never told us": Auditors may not be familiar with the very products that can protect their clients! While the accounting profession does require continuing education for CPAs to retain their licenses, there may not be adequate education on fraud problems and solutions outside of traditional accounting.

In the next chapter, we examine bank lines of credit, a liquidity source that supplements cash.

Summary

The two critical factors in managing cash are float and processing expenses. Float is significant because nearly all business elements have inherent delays that increase costs. Although float cannot be eliminated, every step of the cash-flow timeline should be examined in the search for savings opportunities. Processing expenses are important as each transaction has a cost and an impact on profitability. Both float and processing expenses can be managed through the use of bank products, the most important of which are lockboxing and controlled disbursement. Electronic transactions are managed using Fedwire and the ACH.

CHAPTER 3

Cash, Credit, and Short-Term Financial Instruments

After reading this chapter, you will be able to:

- Consider matching of cash collections and disbursements in an integrated process.
- Understand how to construct cash forecasts and cash budgets.
- Learn about lines of credit and asset-based financing.
- Evaluate how to invest excess short-term funds.

The previous chapter discussed procedures to manage cash as it is received and disbursed. In this chapter, we analyze the choices financial managers have when short-term liquidity requirements do not match cash from operations and bank accounts. The process involves three steps, which we will review in this chapter.

1. Developing a short-term forecast.

2. Preparing a cash budget.

3a. Arranging for a line of credit or other financing for temporary cash deficiencies *or*

3b. Investing any excess cash in securities with short-term maturities.

Developing a Short-Term Forecast

Statistics can be applied to business forecasting through various processes. One technique is regression analysis, which measures how much of a factor (the dependent variable) is caused by other factors (the independent variables). An example is estimating sales based on experience with such causal factors such as advertising, sales calls, and recent sales experience. Another useful technique is time series analysis using the moving-average method, which forecasts future events (like future sales) based on known past events (like recent sales).[1]

The distribution method is a technique that is simple yet useful. With sufficient historical data on patterns of inflows, cash forecasts can be prepared based on day-of-the-week and day-of-the-month patterns of activity. This technique is effective for companies with a fairly regular sales pattern and is helpful in estimating disbursement check clearings.

How to Use the Distribution Method

In order to analyze cash flows using the distribution method, a company must accumulate data on patterns of receipts for at least three or four months. Exhibit 3.1 illustrates a schedule that results from this history, allowing us to predict the receipt of payments for retail sales.

Based on forecast sales for the coming month of June of $500,000, the amount for any particular date can be calculated. Assume that Monday, June 17, is the fifteenth business day (as there is no activity on Sundays). We can forecast the activity of that day using the day-of-the-week factor as adjusted, multiplied by the day-of-the-month factor multiplied by the monthly sales forecast. The adjustment changes the day-of-the-week factor by dividing it by the average day amount; a six-day week is adjusted using 16.667 percent, while a five-day week is

---

1. See any standard text; e.g., William G. Marchal, Robert D Mason, and Douglas Lind, *Statistical Techniques in Business and Economics, 14th edition* (New York: McGraw-Hill, 2010).

EXHIBIT 3.1

Illustrative Distribution Method (by Business Day)

Receipts by Day of the Week		Receipts by Day of the Month	
Mondays	15%	1st, 15th, 30th (includes the 31st)	7%
Tuesdays	10%	2nd, 16th	6%
Wednesdays	15%	3rd, 17th	5%
Thursdays	15%	4th	4%
Fridays	20%	5th, 6th, 7th, 8th, 9th, 10th, 18th	3%
Saturdays	25%	19th, 20th, 21st, 29th	3%
Average day	*16.667%*	All other days	2%

adjusted using 20 percent (100 percent ÷ 5 days). For June 17, the calculation is as follows:

$$(15\% \div 16.667\%) \times 7\% \times \$500,000 = \$31,500$$

This calculation is useful in planning for our daily business activities, but our real working capital need is for cash.

Preparing a Cash Budget

The second step in determining appropriate short-term financing actions is to forecast your cash position through a process known as cash budgeting. While the example that follows uses monthly data, which is acceptable for a small business, many large companies prepare daily cash budgets while those in the middle market prepare such an analysis once or twice a week.

Information Required for the Cash Budget

A cash budget is based on accrual accounting data such as sales, expenses, and other income statement accounts.[2] We convert sales into

---

2. *Accrual accounting* attempts to match revenues (sales) to the costs of developing those revenues. Nearly all large companies use accrual accounting and its conventions, such as depreciation. *Cash accounting*, which is used primarily by small businesses, recognizes revenues as cash is received and expenses as cash is disbursed.

expected cash collections by assigning the historical experience of customer payment histories as applied to actual sales. In a similar manner, we convert expenses into cash disbursements. Then we add non-recurring cash events, including dividends, taxes, capital investments, and similar activities.

Assume that sales and expense forecasts for the Rengas Company are as follows:

	Sales	Expenses
April	$30 million	$32 million
May	$40 million	$35 million
June	$50 million	$43 million
July	$60 million	$52 million
August	$50 million	$43 million
September	$40 million	$35 million
October	$30 million	$30 million
November	$30 million	$28 million

Of course, these are forecasts based on statistical estimates and actual results will vary from our projections.

Assume that all sales are credit, with 20 percent collected in the month of the sale, 60 percent collected in the following month, and the remainder collected in the second following month. All expenses are paid during the month they are incurred; in addition, a tax payment of $4 million is due in July and again in September. The beginning cash balance in June is $6 million.

How to Organize the Cash Budget

We'll prepare a cash-flow statement for June through August (see Exhibit 3.2). Assuming the company's minimum allowable cash balance is $5 million, we'll prepare a surplus–deficit cash projection for those three months. We begin with the cash collections for June, which involve some monies collected that month (20 percent of sales or $10 million), 60 percent of sales in the previous month (60 percent of

EXHIBIT 3.2

Illustrative Cash Budget

($ thousands)	June	July	August	September
Sales	*50,000*	*60,000*	*50,000*	*40,000*
Collections				
That month (20%)	10,000	12,000	10,000	8,000
Month after (60%)	24,000	30,000	36,000	30,000
2 months after (20%)	6,000	8,000	10,000	12,000
Total cash in	40,000	50,000	56,000	50,000
Payments				
Expenses	43,000	52,000	43,000	35,000
Taxes	0	4,000	0	4,000
Total cash out	43,000	56,000	43,000	39,000
Net cash in/out	(3,000)	(6,000)	13,000	11,000
Beginning cash	6,000	3,000	(3,000)	10,000
Ending cash	3,000	(3,000)	10,000	21,000
Minimum cash required	5,000	5,000	5,000	5,000
Surplus/deficit	(2,000)	(8,000)	5,000	16,000
Bank borrowings	2,000	8,000	0	0
Cumulative borrowings	2,000	10,000	5,000	0
Short-term investing	—	—	—	11,000

Note: Accrual accounting data are denoted by italics; all other data are based on conversion to cash accounting.

May's sales or $24 million), and 20 percent of sales in the second previous month (20 percent of April's sales or $6 million). The total of "cash in" for June is $40 million. We can then calculate July through September in a similar manner.

The payments are all made in the month incurred, but we must remember to include taxes of $4 million in July and in September. The total of "cash out" is entered, and the net of "cash in" and "cash out" is calculated, a negative $3 million for June. We began June with $6 million, and we expect to end June and begin July with $3 million. However, our minimum cash is $5 million, so we are "short" $2 million in June.

To obtain this amount, we could arrange for bank borrowings, sell short-term investments, or use other financial strategies. As we work these calculations through the remaining months, we determine total borrowings and the amount available to invest after the borrowings are repaid. What are the options? Arrange to finance $2 million in June and $8 million in July; use the surpluses of $5 million in August and $11 million in September. We'll explore our options in the next sections.

Credit Financing

The next step is the consideration of the various credit arrangements provided by banks (and such other lenders as commercial finance companies), including lines of credit and asset-based financing. We discuss the documentation requirements for such loans in *Tips and Techniques: Arranging for a Bank Line of Credit.*

TIPS AND TECHNIQUES

Arranging for a Bank Line of Credit

When arranging for a line of credit or any type of bank loan, the borrower should come fully prepared to meet with a banker. Essential documents are the cash budget (discussed in this chapter), and pro forma financial statements (an income statement and a balance sheet). The term *pro forma* refers to projected or in the form of, and reflects expected results for coming periods. In addition, bank loan officers require audited financial statements from recent reporting periods.

Other data that should be provided include specific sources of sales, including customer names and their likely purchases; marketing plans including advertising and promotional activities; likely employee hirings and terminations; and justification for major expenses, such as new equipment, the rental of additional production capacity, outsourcing arrangements, and other initia-tives. You should be prepared to discuss contingency arrange-ments in the event that you fail to make your business goals.

Your banker will indicate the frequency and form of the future exchange of data to keep him or her updated on current develop-ments. Any expectations regarding using other bank services, such as the products discussed in Chapter 2, will be suggested. (Because of the illegality of tying arrangements, bankers cannot require that you buy noncredit services in order to obtain credit.) In the interim, maintain contact with the banker—he or she does not want to be unpleasantly surprised!

Lines of Credit

A company may arrange with a bank for access to a line of credit, a spec-ified amount of money accessible for a specified time period, usually one year.[3] The line may be drawn as needed during seasonal shortages of cash resulting from normal operations. In the cash budget example, the Rengas Company needs $2 million in June and $8 million in July, and we could use the credit line to meet those temporary needs.

The bank guarantees the line, if it is committed, so long as the bor-rowers meet all of the conditions of the agreement. An uncommitted line is not guaranteed but is almost always granted (assuming the terms of the lending arrangement are met). Depending on the credit risk and condition of the company, banks will typically charge a fee about 0.5 percent for a committed facility; there is no fee for an uncommitted line. Typical pricing of the used portion of the line is about 2 to 4 per-cent above Federal funds or LIBOR, depending on the perceived credit risk of the borrower.[4]

---

3. Loans for longer periods are known as revolving term loans (sometimes called "revolvers") for peri-ods of one to five years.
4. Federal funds (Fed funds) is the rate that U.S. commercial banks charge each other for overnight borrowing. The London Interbank Offered Rate (LIBOR) represents that arrangement outside of the United States. Many U.S. loans are based on one of these rates.

Restrictions in Lines of Credit

Loan covenants apply to lines of credit and other types of credit agreements, which are restrictions that require a certain level of performance by borrowers. These may include limitations on new debt beyond current borrowings, changes in business strategies or senior management, and various financial compliance requirements, often as measured by standard ratios in such categories as liquidity, leverage, activity, and profitability. See *In the Real World: Bank Returns on Lines of Credit* for a discussion of considerations for choosing between committed and uncommitted lines of credit.

IN THE REAL WORLD

Bank Returns on Lines of Credit

U.S. banks only make positive returns—between 10 and 11 percent—when at least a nominal commitment fee is earned. Uncommitted lines return 6.7 percent after default losses are included, which is just about equivalent to the bank cost of capital (the bank's financing cost).[a] The seemingly illogical decision of banks to provide lines of credit without commitment fees has been due to three factors:

1 Banks' profitability models have been available only since about 1985, and the assumptions in these models are questionable given the strong negotiating position of large corporate borrowers, at least until the present credit crisis. In other words, a strong corporation may negotiate away commitment fees and other loan covenant conditions, while banks have been unwilling to hold the line on cost recovery strategies.

[a] The cost of capital is discussed in Appendix B. The analysis used in this *In the Real World* is in the author's paper, "Bank Transparency: Cost of Capital and Return on Credit Issues," Midwest Finance Association annual meeting, 2010. Contact the author for the complete paper.

❷ In the past, noncredit products have subsidized credit such as those discussed in Chapter 2. Banks may knowingly (or unknowingly) provide no or low return credit products such as credit lines in order to have the opportunity to sell higher return noncredit products.

❸ Credit is profitable for banks for certain groups of companies. These include some middle market and most small businesses, and situations where reasonable returns can be earned in specific industries due to the absence of lending competition.

There is no assurance that banks will be willing to provide free uncommitted lines or committed lines for a nominal fee of 0.5 percent given the recent problems of the banking industry. Furthermore, financial managers do not act prudently when they fail to lock in committed lines. The natural impulse is to bargain aggressively for a reduction in this fee, to shop for better pricing from a competitor, or to accept an uncommitted, "free" line of credit. Bargaining and shopping are certainly acceptable, but settling for an uncommitted line would be a mistake for the following reasons:

❶ In normal economic times, a middle-market business may have a balance sheet comprising total assets of $150 million, with about 10 percent in cash and short-term investments. In addition, lines of credit provide access to financing that represent an additional 5 to 5.5 percent. Assuming current commitment fee pricing of 0.5 percent, the cost of an assured line would be about $40,000 a year. While companies may be reluctant to spend this amount to guarantee access to credit, it should be considered to be as essential for business survival as insurance or risk management.

❷ As noted, banks cannot make an adequate return on uncommitted credit lines, and are beginning to carefully review and expunge those activities and others that do not earn target returns. This is not a new phenomenon; banks have been ending unprofitable relationships for at least

IN THE REAL WORLD (CONTINUED)

two decades. The likelihood is that further terminations will occur.

❸ Credit rating agencies are enhancing their forecasting models to include off-balance-sheet financing such as lines of credit. Acceptable credit ratings are essential to maintaining good supplier relationships, particularly as more vendors look to asset-based financing for working capital, which is subject to lender approval. Your creditworthiness and the agreement of companies to sell to you depend on having a committed line of credit.

Lines of credit are essential sources of liquidity for any business. You do not want to receive a telephone call from your banker that your uncommitted line of credit has been pulled.

In situations where the credit is questionable, the bank may demand collateral and protective covenants to secure the loan. Exhibit 3.3 provides the details of such an arrangement. In this example, the bank has a security interest in leasehold improvements, accounts receivable, inventory, equipment, furniture and fixtures, and all cash and noncash proceeds. In addition, banks require that their borrowers stay out of the bank, that is, not use the line, for a minimum number of months each year, usually two consecutive months, so that the line is not part of its permanent financing.

Asset-Based Financing

Asset-based financing uses a company's accounts receivables and/or inventory as collateral in situations where the lender is uncertain of the borrower's creditworthiness. Typical costs are 4 to 5 percent higher than arranging a line of credit.

- *Factoring* of receivables involves the direct collection from the borrower's customers, who are instructed on the invoice to remit to a specified address controlled by the lender.

EXHIBIT 3.3

Illustrative Bank Loan Agreement

This letter will serve as the offer of XYZ Bank ("Bank") to provide financing on the following terms and conditions:

Purpose:	Working capital line of credit
Amount:	$10,000,000
Maturity:	One year
Interest rate:	Prime rate of bank plus one percent (1%) per annum
Payments:	Monthly payments of accrued interest, outstanding balance and accrued interest due, and payable in full at maturity
Collateral:	A valid, perfected first security interest in all leasehold improvements, accounts receivable, inventory, equipment, furniture and fixtures, and all cash and noncash proceeds thereof, now owned or hereafter acquired by the Borrower
Financial statements:	The Borrower shall furnish to the Bank, within 45 days of the end of each quarter, one copy of the financial statements prepared by the Borrower. The Borrower will also furnish to the Bank, within 90 days of the end of each fiscal year, one copy of the financial statements audited by an independent public accountant. Borrower shall furnish to Bank, within 15 days after the end of each month, an aging of the Borrower's accounts receivable in 30-day incremental agings.*
Financial covenants:	During the term of the note, Borrower shall comply with the following financial covenants:
	Net Worth. Maintain a Net Worth of not less than the sum of $15,000,000 at all times.
	Debt to Assets. Maintain a ratio of Total Debt to Total Assets equal to or less than 40 percent.
Expiration:	This commitment shall automatically expire upon the occurrence of any of the following events:

a. Borrower's failure to close the loan by April 15, 20XX, or such later date as Bank may agree to in writing.

b. Any material adverse change** in Borrower's financial condition or any occurrence that would constitute a default under Bank's normal lending documentation, or any warranty or representation made by Borrower herein is false, incorrect, or misleading in any material respect.

---

*An *aging schedule* shows the quality of a company's receivables by listing the amount of outstanding invoices by groupings of days. A schedule may show a large amount of unpaid receivables more than 30 or 60 days old, which would be of concern to a lender dependent on that revenue source.

**A *material adverse change* is a provision often found in financing agreements (and merger and acquisition contracts) that enables the lender to refuse to complete the financing if the borrower suffers such a change. The rationale is to protect the lender from major adverse events that make the borrower a less attractive client. *(continued)*

EXHIBIT 3.3
(continued)

The foregoing terms and conditions are not inclusive and the loan documents may include additional provisions specifying events of default, remedies, and financial and collateral maintenance covenants. This commitment is conditional upon Bank and the Borrower agreeing upon such terms and conditions.

Oral agreements or commitments to loan money, extend credit, or forbear from enforcing repayment of a debt, including promises to extend or renew such debt, are not enforceable. To protect you (the Borrower(s)) and us (the Bank) from misunderstanding or disappointment, any agreements we reach covering such matters are contained in this document, which is the complete and exclusive statement of the agreement between us except as we may later agree to in writing to modify it.

Additional requirements of the Borrower are as follows:

1. Resolution of the board of directors authorizing the loan.

2. Warranties by the borrower as normally required, including that the business is duly incorporated, that it is not a party to substantive litigation, and that it is current with all tax payments.

- *Inventory financing* is used in industries with expensive equipment and medium-length sales cycles. The lender uses the equipment as collateral, and the loan is paid as sales are made to customers of the borrower.

We will discuss asset-based lending in more detail in Chapters 5 and 6.

Short-Term Investments

In our cash budget, we had excess cash of $11 million in September. This section discusses the final step in our cash decision: examining investments appropriate for any temporary excess of cash. We paid down our borrowing with the excess cash in August for two reasons:

1. It is always more expensive to borrow than to invest, often by 3 or 4 percentage points.

2. The bank expects its borrowers to repay lines of credit as soon as cash is available.

"No Effort Investments" and Equivalents

There are two investment vehicles that do not require any action by the financial manager. While we could just leave any unneeded money in the bank, the earnings we would receive on such "no effort investments" is minimal.

- *ECRs.* The Federal Reserve's Regulation Q prohibits the payment of interest on corporate checking accounts called *demand deposit accounts* (DDAs). While there has been discussion for about two decades of changing this rule, the restriction continues.[5] As a result, banks have long used the concept of the earnings credit rate (ECR), which is applied to average balances left on deposits and used to offset any service charges.

  The calculation is shown on the bank's monthly invoice, called the account analysis. Assuming an ECR of 2 percent, a company would earn $375 for a month on an average earnings balance of $225,000 (see Exhibit 3.4). We will be discussing the account analysis further in Chapter 4.

  Companies that desire to earn this credit simply do nothing, and the bank will automatically apply the earnings against any bank service charges. However, the effective return is only 1.8 percent ($375 × 12) ÷ $250,000 when the ECR is 2 percent. The ECR rate is calculated by the bank against a benchmark rate, usually the yield on short-term U.S. Treasury securities.

- *Sweeps.* Banks and investment companies introduced sweeps in the 1980s, when high interest rates were a strong incentive for financial

---

5. Not-for-profit organizations are exempt from this rule.

EXHIBIT 3.4

Illustrative ECR Calculation (Based on a Typical Bank Account Analysis)

Description	Purpose	Amount
Average ledger balance	Reflects the ledger amount of debits and credit in the bank.	$2,000,000
Less: Average float	Shows the funds in the process of collection through the assignment of availability.*	$1,750,000
Equals: Average collected balances	Indicates the average funds that can be used for transactions.	$250,000
Less: Federal Reserve requirement (currently 10%)	Is the amount set by Federal Reserve rules that banks must hold to maintain liquidity.	$25,000
Equals: Average earnings balance	Shows the amount on which the company earns an ECR credit.	$225,000
Earnings credit rate (ECR)	Applies the current earnings rate.	2%
ECR allowance	Provides the earnings allowance for the month.	$375.00**

*Availability is a bank-assigned factor that reflects the expected number of days required to receive collected funds for checks deposited.
**Calculated as (2% × $225,000) ÷ 12 months

managers to aggressively invest short term. A sweep automatically moves any DDA balances into an interest-bearing account outside of the bank. There is a fairly wide choice of investments for companies that use sweeps, including government and corporate securities and offshore higher yielding opportunities. Balances are returned the next morning to the DDA.

The all-in charge for a sweep account is about $100 a month, so interest income must significantly exceed that cost, which may be difficult in the current low-interest environment. For example, 2.5 percent earned on $50,000 produces only about $100 in monthly interest income and is not worth the effort to create a sweep account. A concern with sweeps is that there is no Federal Deposit Insurance Corporation (FDIC) insurance on the amount swept while it is outside of the bank.

"Some Effort" Investments and Equivalents

Many companies use telephone or Internet instructions to their banks or securities firms to make safe investments with reasonable returns. While financial managers may receive advice, they must actively choose among the instruments and maturities. Furthermore, these investments may charge a transaction fee, and there is a cost for the movement of funds to pay for the investment. See Exhibit 3.5 for short-term investment rates just before the 2008–2009 credit crisis, a period generally considered as "normal," and more recently, an unusual period in our economic history.

- A *banker's acceptance* (BA) is an instrument created when a bank guarantees an international transaction using a letter of credit. The bank sells the BA to investors at a discount and accepts the responsibility for repaying the loan, protecting the investor from default risk. BAs are generally issued for up to six months.

EXHIBIT 3.5

Comparison of Rates in Debt Instruments (Pre- and Post-Credit Crisis)

	Late March 2008	Late March 2010
Federal funds	2.4	0.2
U.S. Treasury Bills	1.4	0.1–0.2
LIBOR	2.7	0.2–0.3
Prime Rate	5.3	3.3
Broker Call	4.0	2.0
Commercial Paper (direct placed)	2.3	0.2
Commercial Paper (dealer placed)	2.6	0.2–0.3
Money Market Mutual Funds	2.0–3.0	0.2
U.S. Treasury Notes	3.0	1.5
U.S. Treasury Bonds	4.0	3.8

Note: There are several published sources of rates on debt instruments, including the *Wall Street Journal*, the *New York Times,* and *Barron's* (in the "Market Week" section and at www.barrons.com/data).

- A *repo* (repurchase agreement) is an investment contract between a brokerage firm or bank and an investor. The repo is sold with an agreement for repurchase at a future date at a set price with most settling overnight. There is minimal risk with repos, although companies interested in this investment should ascertain that there is adequate collateral supporting the repo.

- *Commercial paper* (CP) includes unsecured notes issued by companies with high credit ratings. Maturities are from a few days to 270 days. Most issuers use CP as a continuing financing source and reissue the CP at the time of redemption. Sales are either direct to investors or through dealers (securities firms). Much of the outstanding CP is backed by bank credit lines, minimizing any risk to investors. CP typically carries ratings by leading credit rating agencies and is graded as A-1, P-1, or A-2, P-2.

- *Money market mutual funds* (MMFs) are pools of various types of short-term investments that offer shares to corporate investors. A significant benefit of MMFs is that relatively small units of funds can be placed, allowing the earning of some yield even to the small corporate investor. The diversification in these funds mitigates any risk from the decline in value of a particular holding.

- *U.S. Treasury securities.* Securities of the U.S. government include Treasury bills and notes (those with maturities from 1 to 10 years); and *Treasury bonds*, with maturities from 10 to 30 years. These instruments are highly liquid and risk-free, although the longer the maturity, the greater the risk that inflation could impact the real return.

- *U.S. agencies.* Although not generally well known, there are various federal agencies that issue securities to fund their operations. Two of these agencies are backed by the full faith and credit of the government: Ginnie Mae (the Government National Mortgage Association) and Vinnie Mac (the Department of Veterans Affairs).

Other agencies include Fannie Mae (the Federal National Mortgage Association), Freddie Mac (the Federal Home Loan Mortgage Corporation), and the CoBank ACB, a component of the U.S. farm credit system that funds agribusinesses.[6]

- *Municipal securities.* State and local government municipal securities (munis) have the attraction of having their interest payment exempt from taxes, although yields are less than those of other instruments. The investor has various options in selecting among munis, including revenue securities, which are backed by revenue streams from specific projects, and general obligation securities, which are backed by the income sources of the issuer.

Policies on Short-Term Investing

Many companies have written policies that clearly define acceptable risks, instruments, and maturities for investments. Such policies should reflect the appropriate profile on risk and expectations on return. The purpose of these policies is to protect the company against bad investment decisions and the possible loss of principal. A committee made up of the board of directors and financial managers will normally draft an investment policy. Exhibit 3.6 outlines the issues that an investment policy should address. These are particularly important in the context of the collapse of Bear Stearns in March 2008 and the possibility of the loss of invested funds.

Summary

Financial managers have a sequence of decisions when short-term liquidity requirements do not match cash from operations and bank

---

6. Fannie Mae and Freddie Mac are government sponsored enterprises (GSE) of the U.S. government. As GSEs, they are privately owned corporations authorized to make loans and loan guarantees, with the implied guarantee of the government. The failure of these two agencies in September 2008 forced the Federal Housing Finance Agency to place them under its conservatorship. The eventual disposition will likely be a sale of the assets, a recomposition or nationalization for the purpose of pursuing their mission of providing home ownership to low-income Americans.

EXHIBIT 3.6

Investment Policy Issues

Investment objective	What is the company's acceptable level of risk and yield? How important is yield given the safety of principal and liquidity?
Investment authority	Who is authorized to implement the investment policy and make investments on behalf of the company, and to what limits, and in which instruments?
Audit trails	What type and frequency of reporting and audit trails will be available to monitor compliance with the investment policy?
Permitted or restricted instruments	Which investment instruments are permitted or prohibited in the portfolio? What is the accepted credit quality and marketability?
Maturity	What maturities are acceptable in terms of risk and liquidity?
Diversification of investments	What are the allowable positions in different types of investments with regard to issuers, industry, and the country of the issuer?
Securities dealers	Who are the acceptable dealers with whom the company is prepared to deal? In what amounts?
Safekeeping	What custodial arrangements are required, both to safeguard the company's investment and to facilitate audit requirements?

accounts. These involve developing a short-term forecast, preparing a cash budget, and arranging for a line of credit or other financing for temporary cash deficiencies *or* investing any excess cash in securities with short-term maturities.

Various techniques are available to prepare short-term forecasts; our focus in this chapter was on the distribution method, which uses day-of-the-week and day-of-the-month factors. Cash budgeting restates accrual accounting data to cash accounting terms and then determines the beginning and ending cash for each forecast period. Lines of credit (and other financial arrangements) provide temporary sources of cash during expected deficiencies. Various short-term investment alternatives offer opportunities to earn returns on excess cash, with the choice based on yield, risk, and the effort required to make and manage the investment.

CHAPTER 4

Concentration Banking and Financial Institution Relationships

After reading this chapter, you will be able to:

- Recognize current trends in banking relationship management.
- Understand the concept of concentration banking.
- Appreciate the purpose and use of the request for proposal (RFP).
- Consider how to evaluate and score bank proposals.
- Review issues relating to the pricing of bank services.

Chapters 2 and 3 discussed considerations relating to cash and credit. Those working capital concerns are closely aligned with decisions about banking—which financial institution to use, how to make the selection, how to determine if your prices and services are what your business needs, and how to manage the relationship with your banker. We'll review those issues in this chapter.

Changing Financial Landscape

At some point in your company's history, a bank account was opened that began either a happy or a troubled relationship. Your predecessor may have walked over to the closest bank office, or knew someone from high school who was working at a bank, or asked a friend, relative, or associate for a recommendation. Those days are over; changes in the regulation of financial institutions have completely altered the competitive landscape and, as the result, how your bank treats its customers.

Financial Deregulation

There were prohibitions on interstate banking in the United States from the 1920s until the mid-1990s.[1] Congress also imposed strict limitations on the business activities of banks, with the most restrictive being the forced separation of investment and commercial banking from 1933 to 1999.[2] The current financial services structure of the United States is significantly smaller in terms of the number of institutions; for example, the nearly 15,000 commercial banks of 1980 are now about 7,000.[3]

The friendly neighborhood banker is a relic of this competitive change. Fewer banks, more products, the integration of technology into the delivery of services (see Chapter 9), and the globalization of business have forced banks to merge or become more knowledgeable, and handshakes have given way to a formal relationship. If you are still using your bank from 10 or 20 years ago, it may be time to reexamine the situation. In the next several sections, we review the functions of your primary

---

1. Interstate banking prohibitions were discussed in Chapter 2. There were some exceptions to this prohibition; i.e., Bank of America was "grandfathered" into business activities in several Western states. The Federal Reserve occasionally would permit an exception when a bank was in danger of failing. For example, Citibank was able to enter Illinois when a local Chicago-based financial institution failed and the Fed asked for Citi's help to prevent losses to depositors and borrowers.

2. The Glass-Steagall Act of 1933, separated commercial and investment banking; this law was repealed by the Gramm-Leach-Bliley Act of 1999. As with interstate banking (see footnote 1), exceptions to this prohibition occurred; for example, Merrill Lynch began offering a comprehensive retail financial services product—the CMA account—in 1977.

3. U.S. Federal Deposit Insurance Corporation, The FDIC Quarterly Banking Profile, Historical Statistics on Banking, annually; Statistics on Banking (2009).

bank; later we discuss a process frequently used in reviewing banks and financial institutions.

Bank Relationship Management

Bank relationship management is a comprehensive approach to the bank–corporate partnership, involving all of the credit and noncredit services[4] offered by financial institutions and required by their business customers. Elements of relationship management include:

- Credit arrangements to meet short- and long-term financing requirements.
- Appropriate noncredit services for U.S. and global transactions.
- Reasonable pricing.
- Acceptable service quality.
- Consideration for financial institution risk.

Prior to recent financial deregulation, companies often had several affiliations with several banks to provide the services they required. To some extent, it was a buyer's market, with bankers selling their products through every possible marketing device, including but not limited to:

- Constant calling to build brand recognition.
- Entertainment to build personal contact and a sense of "obligation."
- Aggressive pricing, often at or even below fully loaded costs.
- A regular rollout of new product offerings.
- The intertwining of the bank's systems with the company's systems, to make a separation as difficult as possible.

---

4. Noncredit services are all of the for-fee products offered to corporate customers, including cash management, trust, shareholder services, custody, trade finance, foreign exchange, and derivative instruments.

Twenty-First-Century Banking

The traditional bank calling strategy worked as long as banks could generate adequate revenues from all of their corporate business, particularly because most financial institutions had a poor understanding of profitability by customer or product line. Furthermore, commercial banks were restricted in the use of capital, and could not pursue more lucrative business, such as investment banking or insurance.

The new regulatory environment allows banks and other financial service companies to pursue a much broader range of business opportunities, reducing their reliance on marginally profitable services. Like all for-profit, shareholder-owned companies, banks require a reasonable return on equity (ROE) from each customer and may terminate a relationship if there is little prospect of acceptable returns in the long run.

A proactive relationship management plan is necessary for companies to satisfy their financial institutions and for bankers to justify the business to their management.[5] Review the situation described in *In the Real World: Finance as the Gatekeeper to Banking Services*. Is this occurring at your company?

Concentration Banking

The term *concentration banking* applies to situations where multiple collection and disbursement accounts exist, and cash needs to be mobilized into and funded from a main bank relationship. The concentration or primary bank is the main provider of credit and noncredit services to a company, but other banks may be used in field or office locations due to long-standing relationships or because no national bank yet covers

---

5. In extending credit, banks must allocate scarce capital to support the loan. The Basel II accords require that all lending be supported by senior debt and equity with risk weights for certain types of credit risk. The standard risk weight categories are 0 percent for short-term government bonds, 20 percent for exposures to developed country banks, 50 percent for residential mortgages, and 100 percent weighting on unsecured commercial loans. The minimum capital requirement (the percentage of risk weighted assets to be held as capital) is 8 percent. For additional information, see www.bis.org.

IN THE REAL WORLD

Finance as the Gatekeeper to Banking Services

Bank contact with companies has traditionally been through the treasurer, whose responsibilities include the safeguarding of the cash and near-cash assets of the company. However, access has been extended through other business functions in recent years as banks have broadened their product offerings. Too often, treasury staff remains unaware of the resulting dilution of its responsibility. For example:

- Purchasing and accounts payable are often the entry for e-commerce and purchasing cards.
- The payroll department or human resources may invite discussions concerning the direct deposit of payroll and payroll ATM cards (paycards).
- The investment or real estate departments may be interested in such specialized services as stock loan, custody, and escrow or tax services.
- Systems or information technology (IT) often initiates discussions about any of the more technology-oriented bank services.

Given the current credit environment, it is essential that the finance organization be the gatekeeper for all financial institution contact. This will ensure that an attractive package of profitable business is assembled for the relationship banks, and will prevent unauthorized negotiations or contracting between the company and other banks.

certain regions. Companies in this situation may use one of the U.S. national banks with wide market coverage.[6]

---

6. These banks include Citibank, J.P. Morgan Chase, Bank of America, and Wells Fargo. Their market coverage is extensive but not complete.

Example of industries with a concentration banking structure include retailing and branch offices that require local financial depositories to receive checks, currency, and credit card receipts. As a result, funds often accumulate in collection accounts. In order to use the funds most effectively, the financial manager needs to concentrate the balances.

Funds Mobilization

There are a number of options for a company to move funds into the concentration account.

- *Company-initiated concentration.* Large companies may develop their own concentration reporting systems. The technology used involves computer processing, with automated notification from the local office to company headquarters using specified protocols. For example, the stock brokerage industry uses proprietary systems to report each day's activity at branches. Some of these systems require the branch to input the transit routing numbers[7] of client checks to determine when collected funds will be received at the local depository for inclusion in the concentration amount. Financial managers prepare the concentration wire transfers or ACHs based on a cost-benefit calculation for each method.

- *Standing instructions.* The administrative efforts necessary to concentrate funds can be minimized by the issuance of instructions to the depository or concentration banks to affect transfers based on specific rules. These criteria could be based on:

  - *Frequency:* Daily or any time interval.

  - *Amount:* Any collected funds or only funds exceeding a predetermined target.

7. A transit routing number (or American Banking Association [ABA]) number is the 9-digit MICR-line number found at the bottom of a check. It is used to route a check to the drawee bank, and essentially constitutes an address.

- *Deposit reporting services.* A deposit reporting service (DRS) assists in the mobilization of funds in local accounts to the concentration account. The office manager contacts the DRS through a toll-free telephone number or a point-of-sale (POS) terminal and following a series of prompts, reports the location number, time, and amount of the deposit, and any detail required by the company (such as the coin and currency subtotal).

The DRS accumulates all of the calls for the company, creates an ACH file to draw down the deposited funds, and transmits the ACH through the banking system. The all-in daily cost per location is approximately $1. The effectiveness of a DRS system relies on the local manager to report accurate and timely information. The company can be notified if any branch does not contact the DRS, allowing a rapid follow-up to determine the reason for the failure.

Funds mobilization and concentration systems often are an excuse for an uncontrolled expansion of local bank accounts. For ideas on getting control of this situation, see *Tips and Techniques: Too Many Bank Accounts?*

TIPS AND TECHNIQUES

Too Many Bank Accounts?

Your financial staff may have only limited data on daily receipts and deposits in local accounts. The complexity and cost of a concentration system, including the burden placed on the local office manager for notifying home office and making the deposit, must be weighed against the value of funds transferred. Rather than a minor change to your banking system, it may pay to consider a complete redesign to eliminate local banks and the funds mobilization process.

Companies with more than 25 bank accounts should examine why these accounts are open. Idle accounts often exist that are infrequently used, and their balances can be moved into a concentration account earning a higher return. The idle accounts can then be closed, saving the monthly maintenance charge and other fees. Each idle bank account closed, assuming the balances are $15,000, is worth about $1,500 a year ($1,000 for the value of the earnings and $500 a year for maintenance and other charges). Closing 15 accounts could save between $20,000 and $25,000 a year and more important, significantly reduce the possibility of fraud.

If a credit line is constantly being used for working capital (as discussed in Chapter 3), move money back to the lender whenever there is an excess of cash to minimize interest costs. Having the same bank for credit and cash management services allows excess funds to repay borrowing through an intrabank transfer, saving about 4 percent (the difference between the bank's ECR and the line of credit borrowing cost). These transfers cost about $0.50 and can move on a same-day basis.

Selecting Your Concentration Bank

The importance of carefully selecting your concentration bank cannot be overemphasized. You want a financial institution that has well-trained staff, the right mix of products, adequate credit facilities, and any ancillary services that your business will require to succeed.

- Are you selling in global markets? You will need letters of credit (discussed in Chapter 8).

- Do you want your bank to handle your collection and disbursement activity? You will need lockbox and/or controlled disbursing (discussed in Chapter 2).

- Are you considering outsourcing your payables function? You will need comprehensive payables (discussed in Chapter 7).

- Do you just need good, objective advice? Your banker and the resources that support him or her are critical to businesspeople in these difficult economic times.

Request-for-Proposals

Many companies select a bank through a request-for-proposal (RFP) process. An initial step used by many companies is to issue a request-for-information (RFI) letter to candidate financial institutions. The RFI is used to determine which banks are qualified and interested in providing banking services. A list of potential bank bidders can be developed from previous calling efforts; contacts at conferences and meetings; and referrals from accountants, attorneys, and business colleagues. The responses to the RFI are used to select the banks to be included in the RFP process.

Companies began using RFPs in the 1980s to formalize purchasing decisions that had become too casual. Existing bank and vendor relationships tended to be given extensions of old business and any new opportunities under consideration without a formal bidding process. See Exhibit 4.1 for a list of available banking RFPs.

Issues Covered in RFPs

The RFP is usually organized as lists of questions pertaining to general banking concerns and to specific attributes relating to each service. Specific conditions for contracting services are included. For example, what are the logistics of the bidding process? Who is authorized to speak for the bank and the company? Will the bids be treated with confidentiality?

General issues pertain to any noncredit service being considered. It also applies to the bank's financial stability, creditworthiness, and approach to management of the organization for the delivery of services, quality control, and similar issues. This is the section of the

EXHIBIT 4.1

RFP Templates for Banking Services

Automated Clearing House (ACH)	Paycard (payroll through ATM cards)
Controlled disbursing	Purchasing card services
Custody services	Remote deposit services
Depository services	Retail lockbox
Disbursement outsourcing	Short-term investment management
E-banking and information reporting	
Global treasury services	Treasury workstations
Merchant card services	Wholesale lockbox
	Wire transfer

Source: www.afponline.org/pub/res/brm/rfp/rfp.html. In addition, information on the RFP process is available at www.tisconsulting.com/RFP.htm.

RFP where references should be requested. In this regard, it is useful to require names of companies in your industry that are of equivalent size. While noncredit services should be bid using RFPs, credit facilities are typically handled through a more informal procedure. *See In the Real World: Credit Facilities Provisions* for a description of current practice.

Specific Service Issues

The issues pertaining to each noncredit service will vary by product. Some examples are provided in Exhibit 4.2. See *Tips and Techniques: Thoughtful Use of RFPs* for ideas on the proper procedures for implementing a bidding process.

Review of Pricing

We defined the account analysis and reviewed the earning credit rate in Chapter 3. In this chapter, we'll examine how companies are charged

IN THE REAL WORLD

Credit Facilities Provisions

Credit facilities normally are not bid through an RFP, but are instead simply requested of the financial institution based on past and projected financial statements, a business plan, booked and anticipated sales, and other relevant data. Specific terms offered by lenders include the following:

- Amount of the loan.
- Maturity or duration of the loan.
- Interest rate, usually the prime rate or LIBOR plus or minus 1 percent or more.
- Payment schedule, usually monthly.
- Collateral pledged to secure the loan, usually involving a perfected first security interest in:
  - Leasehold improvements
  - Accounts receivable
  - Inventory
  - Equipment, furniture, and fixtures
- Financial covenants that the company must meet, usually specified as the attainment of minimum balance sheet account and ratio results. For example:
  - A typical balance-sheet account minimum is net worth above $500,000 or some other amount.
  - A typical ratio minimum is net worth-to-total liabilities greater than 2:1.
- Documents that the borrower must provide, including financial statements and other information.

for noncredit services. The lower portion of the account analysis will vary by bank; an illustrative configuration is shown in Exhibit 4.3. It is

EXHIBIT 4.2

Examples of Bank RFP Questions on Noncredit Services

Wholesale Lockbox	**1.** List the bank's schedule for post office pickups of wholesale lockbox mail for weekdays, weekends, and holidays.
	2. Does the bank have a unique five-digit zip code assigned exclusively for receipt of wholesale lockbox items?
	3. Who performs the fine sort per box number, the bank or the post office? If the bank sorts the lockbox mail, describe the mail sorting operation. Include manual and automated handling, ability to read bar codes, and peak volume capabilities.
Controlled Disbursement	**1.** What is the published time at which customers are notified of their daily controlled disbursement clearings? How many notifications of clearings are made each day?
	2. If more than one notification is made, what percent of the dollars and items was included in each notification?
	3. What are the accepted procedures that are used to fund the debit from each day's clearings?
ACH	**1.** What procedures are used to verify accurate and secure receipt of data transmissions through a secure Internet server?
	2. Can the bank automatically redeposit items returned for insufficient or uncollected funds? When items are redeposited, are any entries posted to the customer's account?
	3. What are the hardware/software requirements for PC-based services? Does the application support use of a LAN? Will assistance with software installation be provided?

useful to calculate the complete cost of each noncredit service and to determine if any unusual or incorrect fees are being charged.

Although pricing has long been the consideration in selecting a domestic cash management bank, recent experience has seen a decline in its importance. Some reasons for the decline:

- *Maturity of the product cycle.* Because many bank products are in the mature phase of the product cycle, there is minimal variation in

TIPS AND TECHNIQUES

Thoughtful Use of RFPs

Access to electronic versions of RFPs has greatly eased the process of drafting questions and assuring that important matters are covered. However, many users simply copy and paste from the files in existing RFPs, rather than editing to exclude irrelevant material or writing new, company-specific questions. Furthermore, it is important to include information germane to the company, such as volumes, peak processing days, technology constraints, design of remittance documents, interest in outsourcing, and similar issues. Remember: A full set of RFP responses with accompanying technical specifications and promotional material can print out to more than 1,000 pages!

EXHIBIT 4.3

Bank Account Analysis: Illustrative Noncredit Service Presentation

Service	Reference	Quantity	Unit Price	Price Extension
Account maintenance	1	2	$25.00	$ 50
Deposits—unencoded	2A	140	0.18	25
Deposits—encoded	2B	600	0.12	72
Returned items	3	50	3.00	150
Checks paid	4	400	0.15	60
ACH debits/credits	5	100	0.10	10
Fedwires	6	4	12.00	48
Total charges	7			415
Net due for services	8			$ 40*

*Based on the Exhibit 3.4 calculation of an ECR allowance of $375.00, which has been deducted from Total Charges.

For a directory of over 200 bank services and their standard codes, see www.afponline.org/pub/sc/srvc.html.

(continued)

EXHIBIT 4.3

(continued)

References:
1. *Account maintenance* is the fixed charge assessed to cover the bank's overhead costs associated with a DDA.
2. *Deposits* are checks presented for deposit. *Unencoded* checks do not have the dollar amount encoded in the MICR line; *encoded* checks have been imprinted by the corporate depositor with the dollar amount using an encoding machine. Encoded checks usually have a lower unit price.
3. *Returned items* are checks not honored by the drawee bank, either due to insufficient funds or a stopped payment by the maker.
4. *Checks paid* are disbursements written against the account.
5. *ACH debits/credits* are automated clearinghouse debits and credits to the account.
6. *Fed wires* are same-day electronic transfers of funds through the Federal Reserve System.
7. *Total charges* are the sum of the price extensions for all cash management services.
8. *Net due for services* is the difference between total charges and the ECR allowance based on the balances in the account.

the price charged by most banks. Furthermore, information on pricing is published in the *Phoenix-Hecht Blue Book of Pricing* (www.phoenixhecht.com), making pricing data widely available to all interested parties.

- *Unbundling.* Banks have unbundled pricing for noncredit services, making line-by-line comparisons meaningless. Some banks charge for each specific service, while others include the service in the fee for the underlying product. For example, controlled disbursing may include positive pay, or it may be priced separately.

- *Quality.* It is generally recognized that any quality or service problems relating to a specific bank product can cost many times the price per unit of the service. As a result, the savings of a few cents per item is not important when compared to the cost to resolve an error, a communication, transmission problem, or other bank issues.

RFP Evaluation

Because of the sheer number of potential questions and answers in a set of proposals, it is very difficult to simply read through and make sense of the material. For this reason, one technique that has been helpful is to organize each set of responses into a table, listing the bank names in the columns and the important answers in the rows.

It is necessary to array the responses for each question with the intention of assigning points based on a template of average answers. For example, despite the maturity of the lockbox product, there are often significant differences in the responses. The application of points to these RFP answers allows for the objective ranking of each bank.

Weighted Scoring of Proposals

The final step in evaluating the banks' proposals is to assign weights to each response based on the perceived importance of the question. The total weight should add to 100 percent, but any individual question can have a weighting ranging from a value of 0 percent to as much as 15 or 20 percent. The weights are based on the company's perception of the importance of each question.

An illustrative weighted scoring for lockbox is provided in Exhibit 4.4 for four banks. The responses are displayed as unweighted (that is, the raw point assignments) and weighted (with the value specified for each response applied to the point assignment). The final results show Bank A with 258 points and Bank D with 252 points, which are significantly better than Bank B and Bank C.

These scores allow the company to consider whether the expected results are consistent with the analysis, or if some adjustment in the weightings is necessary. If the results stand, the company should visit the two finalists to ask difficult questions, meet the client team assigned by each bank, and develop a sense for whether the bank wants to be a long-term "partner." Contact all references and probe to see if

EXHIBIT 4.4

Evaluation Score Sheet for Lockbox

	Weight (%)	Unweighted Scores				Weighted Scores			
		Bank A	Bank B	Bank C	Bank D	Bank A	Bank B	Bank C	Bank D
Unique zip code	8	2	0.5	2	3	16	4	16	24
Number of mail pickups at post office	12	2	1	2.5	2.5	24	12	30	30
Quality assurance program	22	2.5	2	1	3	55	44	22	66
Customer service	20	3	2	2	1.5	60	40	40	30
Error rate per 10,000 transactions	14	2.5	1.5	1.5	3	35	21	21	42
Availability assignment	8	3	2	2.5	3	24	16	20	24
Volume for price discount	8	3	1	0	2.5	24	8	0	20
Period of price guarantee	8	2.5	2	3	2	20	16	24	16
Total Weighted Points	100					258	161	173	252

the bank has met its credit and noncredit obligations with its other clients. The scores can also be used to inform the banks that were not awarded the business why they lost to show that your analysis was objective.

Managing Your Banking Relationships

Once the decision has been made, the next activity is to review the contracts your bank(s) will require as an essential part of the relationship. Each service is governed by agreements that address the various requirements of each party to protect both the bank and the company in the event of a dispute. The contracts have been drafted by the bank's attorneys and are based on long-standing precedent as established in the federal banking statutes and the Uniform Commercial Code (UCC) adopted by all states.

Service-level agreements cover terms of service for each cash management product, and will vary depending on specific operating issues. Banks specify standard processing arrangements for the price that is quoted; any variation is considered as an exception, resulting in additional charges. Typical concerns in service agreements include acceptable and unacceptable payee names on checks for lockbox; names of initiators and approvers for wire transfers; approved account signatories; and approved users and access restrictions for treasury information systems.

Banks require these documents to instruct them on how to handle any transactions that are initiated, and to protect themselves in the event of an error or an attempted fraud. Furthermore, customers will be required to indemnify and hold their financial institutions harmless from and against any liability, loss, or costs arising from each service provided. Relationships with banks require that adequate controls be established of files, reports, and systems (for ideas, see *Tips and Techniques: Control of Banking Records*).

TIPS AND TECHNIQUES

Control of Banking Records

Assign the task of updating banking records to a specific manager. Finance staff is often lax in performing this duty. It was previously noted that covenants in loan agreements must be constantly monitored for compliance. Here are other examples:

- Companies often fail to delete approved signatures from their bank's records even though an employee may have long departed the company.

- Lockbox requirements may change, such as new company names or the preferred processing of nonstandard items (such as foreign currency checks), but no one informs the bank.

- Controls may be weak on the use of confidential data and access codes from remote locations. Your financial managers may be entering or downloading this information from home or a branch office, but are there any logs or other controls to protect the company?

It is important to keep such information up-to-date and secure, to protect the company *and* the bank.

Bank Relationship Reviews

Given the partnership orientation of banks and companies, there has been a growing trend toward periodic relationship reviews. The objectives of the review are to:

- Ensure that the relationship is profitable to the bank while providing added value to the company.

- Develop a consultative attitude between the bank and the company to improve current processes and increase efficiencies.

- Deliver quality customer service and the timely implementation of new products and services.

- Understand the future requirements of the company.

The review is typically supported by a document discussing the expectations of each party during the coming period, usually one year, and supported by specific calendar targets. A typical annual review cycle might consist of the following:

- First Quarter: Formal meeting of company management and bank officers to:

  - Discuss the strategic and financial results for the previous year.

  - Outline the next year's goals and objectives.

  - Schedule the implementation of new initiatives.

- Second Quarter: Calling by the bank's relationship manager to:

  - Update the company on service and technology initiatives.

  - Introduce product specialists.

- Third Quarter: Informal meeting of company management and bank officers to:

  - Review the status of the year's goals.

  - Determine which initiatives to emphasize to meet critical objectives.

- Fourth Quarter: Senior-level social event to:

  - Discuss current year.

  - Plan for the next year and beyond.

At each step in the cycle, adjustments can be made by either party to meet the requirements of the partnership between the company and the bank.

Summary

Recent changes in the regulation of financial institutions have altered the competitive landscape and how your banks treat their customers. There are now fewer banks and more bank products, resulting in the development of relationship management as a comprehensive approach to the bank–corporate partnership and involving all of the credit and noncredit services offered by financial institutions. Concentration banking involves situations where multiple collection and disbursement accounts exist and cash needs to be mobilized into and funded from a main bank account. The selection of a financial institution should use a request-for-proposal bidding process, as supported by periodic bank relationship reviews.

PART II

Other Working Capital Accounts— Receivables, Inventory, and Payables

N *ote:* This is the continuation of Widget Manufacturing Case— Part I, which opened Part I of this book. A suggested solution is provided in Appendix A.

Comprehensive Case: Widget Manufacturing Case II

Arnold could not believe that U. R. had the gall to tell him he needed to drastically reduce the company's receivables and to strongly suggest a clearance sale to reduce inventory. Since the founding of Widget Manufacturing, a company that produces and sells privately branded consumer electronics, no inventory sales had ever been held, although there was a period during the late-1970s recession when the price of televisions had to be reduced to move merchandise.

Manufacturing and Banking Activities

Widget's three manufacturing facilities were listed in Part I. The growth of the business is causing Arnold to consider opening a fourth production site, with both Texas and Tennessee under consideration. However, ongoing cash problems have put this idea on hold. There are 10,000 total employees: 5,000 in St. Louis, 2,000 each in Decatur and South Haven, and 1,000 in the home office in Chicago. Each site maintains local vendors and bank relationships for trade payables, payroll, and collections; see Exhibit II.1 for a listing of these accounts.

Collection Activities

The mailroom personnel at each site sort the mail and deliver it to accounts receivable, where envelopes are opened manually and contents are processed. After cash has been applied against customer accounts, the receivables clerks at each location hand deliver the checks to the receivables manager. He or she endorses the checks, prepares a deposit slip, and takes the bundle home for the night to drop the deposit at the bank first thing in the morning, on the way to work.

Arnold had slowly increased the amount of inventory with the belief that many sales were lost because an item was not in stock when a customer requested it. Sales did grow steadily each year, which bolstered Arnold's idea that sales were directly related to larger inventories and lenient credit. In fact, sales had increased by 1.5 times in the last 10 years, but inventory had doubled over that same time period (see Exhibit II.2 for recent inventory and sales data).

Disbursement Activities

As previously noted, Widget maintains payables and payroll activities at each site. Vendors are selected by the local plant manager with advice from his or her supervisors. Maintenance of local vendor relations is considered important. All payables disbursements are by check, using a variety of accounting software systems, with two major payables runs on the 10th and 25th of each month. The clerk handling payables at each site is also responsible for maintaining payroll records and preparing all

EXHIBIT II.1

Bank Account Fees and Balances

Business Unit (Segment) and Site	Purpose	Average Balance	Bank (NB = National Bank)	Monthly Fees
Televisions and radios, St. Louis, MO	Payroll	$1,000,000	Last National Bank of St. Louis	$ 6,000
Televisions and radios, St. Louis, MO	Payables; local collections	900,000	Next-to-Last National Bank	6,000
Wireless telephones, Decatur, IL	Payroll	1,200,000	Almost Last National Bank	5,000
Wireless telephones, Decatur, IL	Payables; local collections	1,100,000	Mediocre National Bank	6,000
Laptop computers, South Haven, MI	Payroll	800,000	Inept National Bank of Michigan	7,000
Laptop computers, South Haven, MI	Payables; local collections	800,000	Epter National Bank of Michigan	7,000
Corporate HO, Chicago, IL	Central payroll	600,000	Second National Bank of Chicago— Account A	6,000
Corporate HO, Chicago, IL	Payables; local collections	600,000	Second National Bank of Chicago— Account B	5,000
Corporate HO, Chicago, IL	Master Account	1,000,000	Second National Bank of Chicago— Account C	7,000
Total		$8,000,000		$55,000

EXHIBIT II.2		
Inventory to Sales ($ millions)		
Year	Inventories	Net Sales
2005	224.2	829.5
2006	246.7	863.4
2007	264.6	894.5
2008	285.2	931.6

checks. Payables checks are signed by that clerk unless they exceed $2,500, in which case the plant manager must also sign.

Central disbursement accounts are maintained at the home office for executive and staff payroll, payables, and miscellaneous expenses. The latter category includes expenses not directly related to the company's business activities, such as interest costs on loans, credit line charges, sales and marketing expenses, corporate airline tickets, and the like.

The weekly payroll is by check drawn on local banks, with the payroll envelopes distributed on Fridays just before lunch. The payables clerk maintains cash in a strongbox for employees wishing to cash their payroll checks. An average of $25,000 is maintained at each site and at the home office for this purpose, which is replenished by a check cashed by that clerk at the bank. These cash funds are occasionally used by executives and salesmen to pay for travel and entertainment expenses. A voucher is prepared to show the withdrawal of funds for such needs, signed by both the plant manager and the payables clerk.

Widget's disbursement system produces a total of 27,500 checks a month: 20,000 for the semimonthly payroll and 7,500 for payables. The all-in cost of the payables checks is $5.00 each. Various ideas have been suggested by the company's bankers and outside auditors to make the disbursement system more efficient, including analyzing computer requirements to reduce computer time and support; renegotiating bank disbursement costs following competitive bidding; and outsourcing most disbursement activities to a bank and/or vendor.

Arnold Sees His Banker

The growth of inventory had seriously depleted the company's cash flow in the past few years. The cash crunch had been managed through increases in a line of credit at the bank, by not taking vendor's cash discounts, and by Arnold reducing his salary and bonus and foregoing his annual vacation. About 40 percent of purchases by Widget were on terms of 1½, net 40, and until this year the cash discount had always been taken. Now payables are almost 50 days past due, and vendors are demanding payment. This situation had forced Arnold to visit his bank to seek additional financing.

U. R. advised Arnold to request the help of an advisor who could help him establish better controls over his working capital. In addition, the present credit line would be extended only if payment were made of the overdue note amount within 90 days. U. R. also suggested that Arnold reduce his inventories and accounts receivable to be in line with the industry. U. R. and Arnold argued over possible remedial actions, with U. R. insisting that cash be raised as the first priority and Arnold wanting to continue his current management style.

Attacking past-due receivables was a particularly difficult point with Arnold, for he realized that he had no stomach for aggressive actions against his customers. Arnold feared that he would offend them if he demanded payment on those past-dues. Widget sold about 60 percent of its sales on terms of net 30, but several customers took advantage of Arnold's good nature (see Exhibit II.3). As he walked the four blocks between the bank and his office, Arnold began to realize that the business was in serious trouble and wondered if things could ever be fixed.

Questions to Consider

Question 3. What changes do you recommend to the inventory management systems? What are the estimated benefits?

Question 4. What is Widget's cost of not taking the vendors' discounts?

EXHIBIT II.3		
Accounts Receivable Aging Schedule		
Days Past Due	**Amount ($ millions)**	**Percent**
0–29	$ 69.5	31.9%
30–59	47.5	21.8
60–89	47.5	21.8
Over 90	53.3	24.4
	$217.8	100.0%

Question 5. What changes do you recommend to the collections and disbursement systems?

Question 6. Based on the information in Exhibit II.4, prepare a cash budget for June through August.

EXHIBIT II.4		
Monthly Forecast of Sales and Expenses ($ millions)		
	Sales	**Expenses**
April	60.0	64.0
May	80.0	70.0
June	100.0	86.0
July	120.0	104.0
August	100.0	86.0
September	80.0	70.0
October	60.0	60.0
November	60.0	56.0

Note: In preparing a cash budget, you will need the following information. All sales are credit sales, with 20 percent collected in the month of the sale, 60 percent collected in the following month, and the remainder collected in the second following month. All expenses are paid during the month they are incurred; in addition, tax payments of $10 million are due in July and in September. From Exhibit I.3 (in Part I), the beginning cash balance on June 1 was given as $8 million.

Question 7. The company's minimum allowable cash balance is $5 million. Using the cash budget you prepared in Question 6, prepare a surplus–deficit cash projection for those three months (June–August). Show cumulative borrowing activity beginning in June. What do you conclude?

Question 8. What should Arnold Parks do?

CHAPTER 5

Accounts Receivable and Working Capital Issues

After reading this chapter, you will be able to:

- Consider appropriate policies and organizing for receivables management.
- Understand how to use ratios and aging schedules in managing receivables.
- Learn about specific receivables issues including sales financing and credit reporting.
- Evaluate terms of sale, invoicing practices, and factoring in receivables decisions.

O ur discussion so far has focused on cash as the first issue to address in managing working capital. This chapter discusses accounts receivable while Chapter 6 reviews inventory; these are the two significant current asset accounts besides cash. Finally, in Chapter 7 we review accounts payable, the major working capital current liability.

Managing receivables would appear to be a relatively simple matter: send out a bill and hope that payment is made. If not, plead, threaten, or when all else fails, sue! However, the float consequences of poor receivables management are potentially so devastating that this should be a high priority for your company. With cash, we measured float improvement in days. With receivables, it is often measured in weeks.

Elements of Receivables Management

There are various important elements in establishing a program to manage accounts receivable, including establishing policies and organizing your business for the implementation of these policies, both of which are discussed in this section. We will then explain how to monitor results. Many companies have some components of this receivables program. However, the typical situation is that there has been little review or change to long-established procedures, and this inattention may not be costly given the current difficult business climate.

Developing Receivables Policies

Policies on receivables formalize decisions on the extension of credit to customers. Rules should be established on various issues.

- How much credit will be granted to specific groups of customers?

- What are the credit terms that will be extended? That is, how many days will be the standard for payment of invoices or statements?

- Will discounts—called *cash discounts*—be granted for early payment? Will other types of discounts be offered?

- How will the company pursue slow and non-payors? What mechanisms will be used, and what will trigger each action?

- What forms of financing will be used to assist our customers in making purchasing decisions?

- Should we use a financial intermediary to lend to us on our receivables while we await payment in a process called *asset-based lending*? Should we sell our receivables—called *factoring*?

- Are we monitoring our company's salespeople to prevent their making unauthorized credit promises to customers in order to generate sales?

- Should we use the services of a debt collection agency?

Written policies assure consistency in decision making and avoid the possibility of discrimination against certain customers. In situations where preferential treatment is extended, the policy should specify the conditions for such treatment; as when a business relationship has existed for five or more years, or when a customer is consistently current on its payments. Similarly, when punitive treatment is indicated, there should be a policy. For example, a customer consistently late in paying could be disciplined by requiring some cash in advance or by executing a lien on certain assets such as the inventory or equipment that was delivered.[1]

Furthermore, policies establish required practice for all parties that cannot be modified except by senior management. This is important when a customer or a prospect asks for special terms, such as a longer time to pay or a smaller down payment. Any violation should be considered as a serious breach of behavior triggering appropriate penalties. For situations where this can occur, see *Tips and Techniques: Getting to Know You—Getting to Know Your Company!*

---

1. A *lien* is a legal claim that attaches to property. A creditor who holds a lien can often have property sold to satisfy the lien.

Getting to Know You—Getting to Know Your Company![a]

If you are a financial manager, have you recently gone on customer calls with your salespeople? Do you have any idea of what they may be promising to win business; for example, are they offering pricing concessions, lenient credit terms, or a delay in payment? Salespeople are usually compensated by commission or a salary and a bonus for superior performance. Commissions and superior performance are driven by sales and not by concern for profits. Without adequate supervision, sales could be occurring at the expense of financial returns.

Incidentally, manufacturing often responds to the same motivation—production at the expense of efficiency and profitability. Unfortunately, these functional areas typically do not coordinate their decisions except at the level of the company president, and real turf wars can inhibit cooperation and appropriate procedure. Leave the "friendly confines" of your finance office and go on a few sales calls and tour the factory floor. You may be surprised at what really goes on!

---

[a] With apologies to Rodgers and Hammerstein.

Organizing for Receivables Management

Does your company have a receivables manager? Probably not, because most businesses divide that responsibility among each of the parts of the collections timeline that affects receivables: sales (in marketing), credit and collections (also in marketing), invoice generation (probably in information technology), cash receipt (in finance), and cash application (in accounting). While this traditional approach is acceptable, it does not deal with the interrelationship of the various functions to accomplish optimal efficiency.

Calculating Receivables Float

An electronics company billed $500 million per year in mailed invoices prepared through two information systems. Billing terms are "net 30," that is, payments are considered late if received more than 30 days after the invoice is received by the customer. Consistent with industry practice, no cash discounts are offered.

Weekly system runs print invoices an average of 15 days after the sale date. The due date for payment is 30 days after the target date for the customer to receive the invoice (the "customer invoice receive date"). Given typical mail times in the geographic areas served by the company, customers receive these invoices approximately 12 days prior to the due date. The timeline sequence for a typical transaction involving these events is as follows:

- Sale of product: April 1.
- Target issuance of invoice: As soon as possible after April 1, assume April 6.
- Target customer receipt of invoice: April 9.
- Actual issuance of invoice: April 15.
- Actual customer receipt of invoice: April 18.
- Target date to receive payment: May 6.
- Actual due date: May 28.

The slippage or float lost between the target and actual due dates is 22 days. The value of the lost days, at an assumed 10 percent cost of capital, is calculated as:

$500 million × 22 lost days

360 calendar days × 10 percent cost of capital

= $3.1 million.

Research determined that the delay in invoicing was caused primarily by various scheduling issues within the information technology function, with invoicing cycles running at weekly intervals at the convenience of that department.

Once senior management became aware of the potential value of the lost float, it was a relatively simple matter to mandate the rescheduling of processing runs. While some customers did notice the change in the timing of their monthly invoices and held checks until the usual release date, many paid once the bill was approved.

Consider the *In the Real World: Calculating Receivables Float* situation. The various steps in the receivables cycle result in a loss of more than three weeks and $3 million a year, yet no one function is responsible. The rational CEO would demand that this situation be fixed, but who would he or she turn to? Unfortunately, the answer is a group of managers (probably vice presidents), each of whom could blame the others. What is needed is a dedicated senior manager who can analyze the situation and initiate whatever changes are required, from earlier assembly of invoice data (perhaps a marketing or receivables function) through the issuance of invoices (an information technology function).

The receivables manager would also be responsible for specific activities that assist marketing, such as sales financing and cash or trade discounts; that trigger the receivable, including invoicing; and that provide working capital to the company as it awaits payment, such as factoring. In the absence of a receivables manager, your company could establish a task force or committee on receivables with the power to examine and decide on possible changes in procedures.

Receivables Cycle Monitoring: Ratios

In some instances, it is relatively easy to determine if your company is attaining acceptable results. For example, did we eliminate the 22 days of float of the *In the Real World* company? We can develop logs of invoice dates and mailings, and determine if all of the appropriate functions are cooperating. In other cases, we will need to manage our company against the performance of others in our industry to attempt to meet or beat our peers. There are two types of analyses that are useful in this monitoring effort: receivables ratio analysis and the aging schedule.

Receivables Ratio Analysis

You may recall that ratios were discussed in Chapter 1, using receivables turnover (calculated as credit sales ÷ receivables) and a variation of that ratio, average collection period (calculated as receivables ÷ daily credit sales). In comparing ratios, we noted that we would measure the company's result to that of its industry using the interquartile range as normal. Our calculation for receivables turnover was 5.5 times and for average collection period was 66 days.

Now let's examine an actual set of ratios using a standard source; as an example, we'll use plastics manufacturing (NAICS 326121-22).[2] As reported by RMA for 2008–2009, receivables turnover (in turns) was 11 (third quartile), 9 (median), and 7 (first quartile); average collection period (in days) was 32, 43, and 55. This means that results outside of the 11 to 7 turns or the 32 to 55 days should be reviewed for its inadequate performance.

Interpretation of Receivables Ratios

Certainly our results fall well outside of that range (at 5.5 turns and 66 days), but are they due to insufficient sales (the numerator) or poor receivables management (the denominator)? Because receivables directly result from sales, the culprit is certainly receivables management. But is

2. Ratios are provided by industry in the standard sources noted in Chapter 1. For our purposes, we are simply choosing one industry of the some 600 that are reported by RMA. NAICS is the North American Industry Classification System, the standard used by Federal statistical agencies in classifying business establishments for the purpose of collecting, analyzing, and publishing statistical data related to the U.S. business economy. For further information, see www.census.gov/eos/www/naics.

the problem throughout receivables, or is it caused by a small subgroup, likely the slow-paying and nonpaying group of customers?

It should be noted that for most ratios we would have to carefully analyze every ratio among the significant ratios to draw firm conclusions about the source of a problem. For example, a poor current ratio can result from problems with current assets, current liabilities, or both. With receivables, summarized balance-sheet data may mask collection problems with certain customers. The solution is to review an aging schedule.

Receivables Cycle Monitoring: The Aging Schedule

The ratios that we examined are aggregated numbers, that is, they include customers who are current in their remittances (whether early or on time) and those who are delinquent (whether slow, very slow, or not paying at all). An aging schedule is a useful method to determine the extent of each of these practices, and follows the expectation that the longer a bill is unpaid, the less likely it will ever be paid.

The procedure is relatively simple:

- Sort accounts receivable by age, such as in groupings of months unpaid.

- Total the sorted groups.

- Multiply the totals by a factor representing the likelihood of payment, based on previous experience.

Assume that there are five major customers with a recent payment history as shown in Exhibit 5.1. The application of the expectation (probability) of payment calculation is in Exhibit 5.2.

Interpretation of the Aging Schedule

The result is an aging schedule that provides a reasonable estimate of doubtful accounts, which are subtracted from accounts receivable on the balance sheet to arrive at a net figure. In addition, payment patterns

EXHIBIT 5.1

Receivables Aging by Customer

Days Outstanding	0–30 Days	31–60 Days	61–120 Days	121–182 Days	Over 6 Months	Receivables Balance
Anchovy, Inc.	$200,000	$200,000				$ 400,000
Cheese Brothers					$100,000	100,000
Onion Company			$150,000	$150,000		300,000
Pepperoni Group	400,000					400,000
Sausage, Ltd.	300,000	200,000	100,000		50,000	650,000
Total	$900,000	$400,000	$250,000	$150,000	$150,000	$1,850,000

EXHIBIT 5.2

Receivables Aging by Group with Estimated Doubtful Accounts

	Total in Each Aging Group	Percent Doubtful*	Total Doubtful in $
0–30 Days	$900,000	1.5%	$ 13,500
31–60 Days	$400,000	4.0%	16,000
61–120 Days	$250,000	12.0%	30,000
121–180 Days	$150,000	25.0%	37,500
Over 6 Months	$150,000	50.0%	75,000
Total Doubtful (in $)			$172,000

*Based on previous accounts receivable experience

are revealed by customer and when compared against previous results by aging group to show improving or deteriorating experience.

For example, the $150,000 in the 121 to 180 days group is about 8 percent of all receivables. If the previous report showed that group at 6 percent, we'd assume that the credit and collection manager was becoming less aggressive about pursuing overdue payments. And if similar statistics are found elsewhere in the aging schedules, that could be the source of the poor ratio performance.

Aging helps to determine if a company's credit analysis is being properly handled, or if exceptions have become too frequent. A credit report (to be discussed later in this chapter) may suggest that a good customer is becoming slow in paying others, but the marketing manager has not noticed a fall in its credit rating, or may want to help the customer and not lose sales. However, you may be shipping to a customer who will never pay if its business situation has deteriorated.[3] Finally, aging identifies specific problems that are difficult to see in aggregated ratios.

Sales Financing

Sales financing assists customers that may require credit assistance or long payment terms in their purchase activity—with an interest charge— particularly when the product involves a considerable cash outlay.[4] In those situations, sales financing (or leasing) programs, more than pricing or product features, can determine success or failure in making the sale.

Financial managers should be involved in sales financing in the development of pricing models based on timing of payment, anticipated charges (such as late payment fees), and the spread earned on finance charges over the cost of capital. Transaction specifics include the credit terms and interest charges offered to customers and depend on customer creditworthiness, the life of the asset, and industry experience with financing programs.

Although maintaining the overhead of an internal sales financing program can be a significant expense, a major benefit is the ability to

---

3. It is sobering to note a few of the established U.S. companies that recently declared bankruptcy: Linens 'n Things (small appliances), Circuit City (electronics), Fortunoff (jewelry and home furnishings), and Bennigan's (restaurants).

4. Examples of sales financing include automobile and truck dealers (e.g., through GMAC or Ford Motor Credit), aircraft engines and electrical machinery (e.g., through GE Capital), and industrial equipment (e.g., through CIT Group).

directly control response time and deal particulars for each transaction considered. Certain customers may be especially desirable given their business potential or cache, justifying a coordinated sales financing effort. Other customers may be repeat business and the level of effort may be less demanding.

Outsourcing Sales Financing

If this is too difficult, the sales financing process can be outsourced to a finance company or other lender in three possible formats:

1. Full recourse sales financing (allowing lowest interest rates), with the lender becoming the source of funds and offering advice on customer creditworthiness.

2. Limited liability or ultimate net loss, allowing a limitation on the extent of the recourse, with the seller and lender each absorbing some credit risk.

3. No risk, with the lender independently determining the creditworthiness of the customer.

When lenders assume some or all of the risk, approvals can be delayed up to a few weeks, depending on the information provided by the customer and his or her credit rating.

While an outsourcing program avoids certain credit group and legal overhead, customer service could be adversely affected. Certain lenders focus on transaction activity, and may not understand the importance of service to the customers of the selling company. Problems might arise when questions are directed to the lender regarding such matters as the logistics and crediting of payments.

Credit Reporting

Credit information services provide numerical grades of the creditworthiness of companies based on experience reported by vendors and other parties in a business relationship. In making credit sales to a company, the goal is to find evidence of stability, creditworthiness, and the capacity to meet its obligations. Credit report grades are based on the time to pay and amount of recent transactions, as supported by financial statements, public records, liens, lawsuits, number of years in business, and management.

The primary providers of this service are Dun and Bradstreet (D&B), Experian, and Equifax, with reports available on businesses in North America, Europe, and selected Asian countries. Associated marketing analytics include data on customer requirements and typical purchase activity. The credit reporting industry is a huge, sophisticated business; for example, Equifax had revenues in 2008 of $2 billion.

Reporting on Business Creditworthiness

Reporting data include a complete dossier on a company's credit and business history, and a credit score based on a complex proprietary statistical model. While the score simplifies the credit decision down to a single number, it is often too ambiguous to enable a simple "sell or don't sell" decision. In our illustration (Exhibit 5.3), the score is 55 (medium risk), making the credit or "no credit" decision a judgment call.

EXHIBIT 5.3

Business Credit Report

Summary of Business Activity

Key Personnel

SIC Code/Description

Business Type

Experian File Established

Experian Years on File

Years in Business

Total Employees

Sales

Filing Data Provided by SOURCE

Date of Incorporation

Recent Credit History (DBT = Remittances Paid in Days Beyond Terms)

Current DBT

Predicted DBT (for next period)

Average Industry DBT

Payment Trend Indicator

Lowest 6-Month Balance

Business Inquiries

Highest 6-Month Balance

Current Total Account Balance

Highest Credit Amount Extended

Median Credit Amount Extended

Credit Score

55 (Medium Risk)—A credit score predicts payment behavior, with high risk (approaching 100) indicating that there is a significant possibility of delinquent payment, and low risk (approaching 0) meaning that there is a good probability of on-time payment.

Credit Trend Charts (Changes in Payment History Over Time)

Monthly and quarterly payment trends

Continuous, newly reported and combined payment trends

Trade payment experiences by vendor category

Actions on collection disputes including judgments, by date and amount

Fixed debt obligations (such as leases)

Note: These credit and business history categories are similar in all three credit reporting companies. For a sample report, see www.experian.com/small-business/businessreport/samples/businessCreditAdvantageReport.jsp.

The assemblage of required data could not be accomplished by any company at any price, and so many businesses subscribe to and use these services. Individual reports typically cost about $40, and subscriptions start at about $50 a month. To review your company's credit situation, see *Tips and Techniques: Fixing Your Company's Credit Score.*

TIPS AND TECHNIQUES

Fixing Your Company's Credit Score

In Chapter 3 we discussed various sources of credit for your company. This chapter discusses your customer's credit scores. Just as you are vitally concerned about the credit scores of your customers, you should pay attention to your own company's scores. Here are several recommended steps:

- Check the credit report of your business regularly and verify that the information in it is accurate and up-to-date.

- Establish credit with businesses that report trades. Not all business creditors report their trade information so you will have to make inquiries.

- Pay your creditors on time; past payment behavior with vendors plays a major role in calculating your business credit score.

- Remember that credit scoring uses several variables in its calculation, and none of the mathematics is disclosed. You should try to manage everything, but most particularly outstanding balances; your payment habits; the extent of credit used; actions against your company for collection; and demographics such as years on file, Standard Industrial Classification codes,[a] and business size.

---

[a] A Standard Industrial Code (SIC) is a 4-digit code assigned to each industry by the U.S. Department of Commerce for classification purposes. It has recently been supplemented by the 6-digit NAICS code.

Terms of Sale

Vendors normally follow industry practice in establishing terms of sale, which is the length of time allowed before payment is expected. Terms are stated as "net" and the number of days, usually beginning on the date of the receipt of the invoice or statement, as in "net 30" or "n30." Terms follow the normal selling cycle of a business, so companies that require about 60 days to sell goods would receive terms of "net 60."

Cash Discounts Basics

Although many texts discuss cash discounts, actual experience today is that less than 10 percent of vendors offer such price reductions to their customers. The discount is specified as the amount of the discount and the last date on which the discount is offered. The cash discount "2/10" means that 2 percent may be deducted from the invoiced amount, but payment must be received no later than 10 days after the bill is received. A full set of commonly used terms is "2/10, n30." Terms are printed near the top of the invoice or statement.

The selling company and its customer should be aware of the value of the cash discount in order to decide on appropriate decisions. Terms of "2/10, net 30" calculate to 36 percent of value annually, determined as follows:

- Calculate the "nondiscount" days in the credit cycle; e.g., 30 days − 10 days = 20 days.

- Divide the result into 360 days; e.g., 360 days ÷ 20 days = 18 annual payment cycles.

- Multiply the number of cycles times the cash discount; e.g., 18 cycles times the 2 percent cash discount = 36 percent,[5] which is the annual value of the discount.

---

5. The actual calculation is $(2\% \div 98\%) \times (18) = (.0204) \times (18) = 36.72\%$. This assumes a 360-day year. A 365-day year results in a rate of 41.37%.

- Compare the annual discount to the cost of capital; e.g., 36 percent (the value of the discount) versus 10 percent (the cost of capital we've used throughout this book).

Cash Discount Decision Factors

In this situation, we would take the discount if we were customers, as it is more than $3^1/_2$ times the cost of capital. However, the selling company should not offer such a generous incentive, as its financial cost is likely far greater than any sales benefit. Another consideration is that any customer regularly taking the discount and then passing it might be suspect to the vendor, who may assume that the customer's financial situation has deteriorated.

Cash discounts create a dilemma for companies when their customers take the discount but pay after the discount period. Should the customer be billed for the discount or should the policy infraction be ignored? If this is ignored once, the customer will simply repeat its action with each invoice. If the customer is billed for the discount, bad feelings could result.

Other Discounts

The most common types of discounts offered to induce customer sales are noted in Exhibit 5.4. However, none of these improve working capital management and, in fact, may result in reduced cash collections.

Invoice Generation

Invoice generation is usually a shared responsibility of sales, receivables, and information technology, with critical decisions on invoice design and the timing of the billing cycle often made at the convenience of systems managers. Invoice runs may be scheduled when time is available in the processing cycle without regard to the optimal timing of the printing and mailing process.

Discounts other than Cash Discounts

There are various types of discounts offered to motivate customer purchasing. The two most important discounts (other than cash) for business-to-business transactions are those based on trade and on quantity (volume).

- *Trade Discounts.* These are payments to wholesalers, retailers, and other members of a marketing channel for performing a marketing function. For example, a trade discount 18/10/4 would indicate a 18 percent discount for warehousing the product, a further 10 percent discount for shipping the product, and an additional 4 percent discount for stocking the shelves. Trade discounts are most frequent in industries where retailers hold the majority of the power in the distribution channel.
- *Quantity Discounts.* These are price reductions given for large purchases. The rationale is to obtain economies of scale and pass some of these savings on to the customer. In some industries, buyer groups and cooperatives have formed to take advantage of these discounts. The two types of quantity discounts are:
  1. *Cumulative Quantity Discounts:* Based on purchases over time.
  2. *Noncumulative Quantity Discounts:* Based on the quantity of a single order.

Invoice Design

Simplifying the invoice or statement eliminates unnecessary verbiage and multiple addresses. A bill should be easy to read and pay, with a clean look. A single return address forces the customer to mail payments to the proper address rather than to a location that may delay processing. (One company had four addresses on each bill—the home office, the regional office, the office of the sales representative, and the lockbox address! Little wonder that many items were sent to the incorrect location.)

Invoice design may involve developing formats readable by automated equipment, including those in magnetic ink character recognition

(MICR) and optical character recognition (OCR) fonts. MICR and OCR are fonts or print characters that have a distinctive design recognizable by automated reader-sorter equipment. MICR and OCR characters are printed in special ink at designated positions on checks and remittance documents, usually at the bottom of the page.

Invoice and Statement Timing

Research has been conducted over the past few decades examining alternative invoice or statement mailing dates and the resulting payment "receive" date for both corporate and retail payments. For most industries, the optimal time for the customer to receive a monthly invoice or statement is 25 days prior to the due date for receipt of funds by the date due. However, many companies are sending bills 10 to 15 days later than optimal, say two weeks prior to the due date, with the result that their days' sales outstanding (DSO) is longer than average for their industry. Equivalent relationships hold for industries billing on cycles other than monthly.

There are several factors that drive this situation:

- The invoice or statement must be received at the correct location (see the comment above on "invoice design") and forwarded to a payables clerk.

- The payables clerk must verify that the invoice or statement is correct. While we defer discussion of the payables cycle to Chapter 7, it is sufficient to note that time is required to gather the necessary purchase order, receiving report, and other documents or approvals.

- Any disputes must be manually entered and deducted from the net payment.

- The approved invoice or statement must enter the disbursement cycle, which runs twice a week in many companies.

The total time that has elapsed can be longer than two weeks. By the time the check is received and collected funds are credited, three weeks may elapse, meaning effective payment is one week later than the due date.

Invoices versus Statements

Some companies issue both invoices and monthly statements. Unless requested by your customers, delivering multiple types of bills can confuse accounts payable clerks, particularly when there is a disagreement in your documents, and may provide an excuse for delaying remittances. Choose one of these forms of billing, basing your decision on industry practice and customer preference, and drop the other type.

Asset-Based Financing: Receivables

Asset-based financing (ABF) became an important supplement to normal bank credit during the credit crisis that began in 2008. It is currently estimated that $750 billion of such lending is outstanding in the United States. Participants include large banks, regional and smaller banks, and commercial finance companies. The two primary assets used in these programs are receivables (discussed in this section) and inventory (discussed in Chapter 6).

Lenders need to understand the collateral at stake and the characteristics of the industry. ABF bankers are in contact with their clients nearly every day and many of them spend time in the field checking up on their clients and their collateral. Cooperation by the information technology function is essential in feeding data on receivables (or inventory) to lenders so that precise data is available on whether credit sales have been paid (and which items have been sold).

Receivables Factoring

Factoring involves the sale of accounts receivable.[6] By selling your invoices for future payment, you generate cash sooner than if you waited

---

6. However, see the previous section in this chapter on "Outsourcing Sales Financing" for recourse versus nonrecourse alternatives. Marginal credit risks may be rejected by a factor, leaving the sales/credit decision to the selling company.

to collect cash from your customers. The factor that purchases your receivables takes title to the invoices and directs that payment be made to a post office box (usually a lockbox) when due. Factoring is expensive, because the cash paid for a receivable is discounted by about 5 percent.

Aging is important in receivables financing, as the older the account, the less value it has. For example, lenders may lend 80 percent of the face value for outstandings less than 45 days old but only 50 percent on older receivables. A monthly interest rate on receivables is calculated by applying a daily percentage rate to the receivables outstanding each day.

As in sales financing, a possible consideration in factoring is harm to customer relations, as any collection actions taken may endanger an ongoing business relationship with one of your customers. There may be situations where you would compromise a debt, extend payment deadlines to a preferred customer, or employ a more lenient collection approach for a specific customer. A factor has little interest in preserving your future relationship with the debtor. See Exhibit 5.5 for a list of factors.

EXHIBIT 5.5

Representative Factoring Organizations

Aquent

Barclays PLC

BB&T Corporation

CIT Group, Inc.

Marquette Financial Companies

Natixis

Wells Fargo Trade Capital

EXHIBIT 5.6

Representative Debt Collection Agencies

Asset Acceptance Capital Corp.

Chamberlin, Edmonds & Associates, Inc.

Encore Capital Group, Inc.

ER Solutions, Inc.

Green Tree Servicing LLC

NCO Group, Inc.

Policy Studies Inc.

Portfolio Recovery Associates, Inc.

Transcom WorldWide S.A.

West Corporation

Debt Collection Agencies

A *debt collection agency* pursues payments on unpaid debts owed by individuals or businesses. Few companies operate their own debt collection activities for accounts older than 90 days. In that situation, a third-party collector is recommended to pursue your "no pay" customers. These firms typically accept assignments on a contingency fee basis, and receive a fee—typically 15 percent—only on amounts received. See Exhibit 5.6 for a list of leading debt collection companies.

Summary

Managing accounts receivables involves establishing policies and procedures and organizing your business for their implementation. An aging schedule is a method to determine the effectiveness of these practices, and follows the expectation that the longer a bill is unpaid, the less likely it will ever be paid. Credit information services provide numerical grades of the creditworthiness of companies based on experiences reported by vendors and other parties in business relationships.

Vendors normally follow industry practice in establishing terms of sale, which is the length of time allowed before payment is expected, with terms stated as "net" and the number of days (as in "net 30" or "n30"). Invoice generation is usually a shared responsibility of various company functions, with critical decisions on invoice design and the timing of the billing cycle often made suboptimally at the convenience of information technology. Asset-based financing based on receivables ("factoring") is now an important supplement to traditional bank credit.

CHAPTER 6

Inventory and Working Capital Issues

After reading this chapter, you will be able to:

- Consider appropriate policies and organization for inventory management.
- Understand how ratios and other metrics assist in inventory management.
- Learn about problems in purchasing and work in process.
- Evaluate new techniques such as EOQ, JIT, and SCM.
- Review such financing alternatives for inventory as asset-based lending.

I n Chapter 5, we noted the many issues involved in managing a seemingly simple working capital activity, accounts receivable. You saw that the process is far more complicated than sell and wait for payment. Managing inventory as a part of current assets is similar in that finance managers typically do not become involved in inventory decisions, which is traditionally the responsibility of manufacturing. Furthermore, the concept of "inventory" makes sense on the balance sheet but is too vague in dealing with the realities of working capital issues. There are two aspects of inventory management:

1. The purchasing of materials and components.

2. The management of those materials and components as they are retrieved and used to produce goods for sale, referred to as *work in process* (WIP).

Various economic and financial factors should be considered in managing inventory, including economic order quantity, that is, how much should be ordered at any particular time; price, volume purchasing, and the possibility of pricing concessions; the timing of delivery of material prior to the beginning of manufacturing; and various other considerations that have come to be integrated into the concept of supply chain management (SCM), which we will define shortly.

Elements of Inventory Management

As with receivables, there are important elements in establishing a program to manage inventory, including establishing policies, organizing for policy implementation, and monitoring results.

Developing Inventory Policies

Inventory policies formalize decisions on the acquisition and use of inventory, and the write-off or scrapping of stale inventory. Rules should be established on several issues, including the following:

- Who is managing our purchasing? Should this function be handled on a decentralized or centralized basis?

- How strictly will we require adherence to inventory and purchasing cycle documentation such as purchase orders (POs) and receiving reports?

- How aggressively should inventory be managed? That is, should we consider a just-in-time (JIT) approach, or is it more prudent to maintain a reasonable amount of inventory of raw materials, WIP, and/or finished goods?

- How forcefully will we address vendor errors? Should we demand some control and/or access to our vendors' sites and procedures, or simply request replacements and/or billing credit?

- Should we allow vendors to buy lunches, drinks, or similar entertainment for our purchasing staff? If this is allowed, what limits are appropriate?

- Should we attempt to forecast our inventory requirements, or is purchasing as our needs are determined adequate to deal with possible price increases or shortages in the future?

- Would using a supply chain management system enhance our ability to compete and satisfy our customers?

Policies establish required practice for all parties that cannot be modified except by senior management. This is important when a vendor offers a special accommodation, when POs and/or receiving reports are not prepared, when faulty materials are delivered, and in many other situations directly affecting manufacturing quality and delivery promises. Any violation should trigger appropriate responses by management.

Organizing for Inventory Management

Optimal inventory management requires a dedicated manager or a task force approach. Unfortunately, most companies defer to purchasing and production managers in making decisions regarding inventory acquisition and use. However, there are large float and cost implications of inventory, and inappropriate decisions or inefficient procedures can add significant costs, adversely impacting working capital. Your company should consider appointing a senior inventory manager or a task force comprised of manufacturing, marketing, finance, and information technology.

Inventory Cycle Monitoring: Ratios

In Chapter 1, we calculated the inventory turnover (cost of goods sold ÷ inventory) of the Rengas Company as 6.7 times; its variation inventory turnover (360 days ÷ inventory turnover) was 54 days. Continuing the actual data for the interquartile range for plastics manufacturing from RMA,[1] we find that the result is 10 (third quartile), 7 (median), and 5 (first quartile) turns and 35, 52, and 76 days. Our company (at 6.7 turns and 54 days) is close to the median result for both ratios. Good news—right? A closer look may be in order, as both of these ratios aggregate considerable data. All of inventory is included, and cost of goods sold—where inventory is placed on the income statement—is the second largest account after sales.

Supplemental Data

There are several additional data that should be examined.

- *Common-size financial statement data.* RMA (and some other sources like *Troy's Almanac*) publish data by industry that sets total assets (and total liabilities and owners' equity) equal to 100 percent, allowing the calculation of the percentage for each significant account. Inventory is 24.9 percent of total assets for this industry, while our company has 12.0 percent in inventory ($15,000,000 ÷ $125,000,000).

- *Additional ratio data.* *Troy's Almanac* publishes ratios that support additional analysis of the basic ratios. For inventory, an inventory-to-working capital ratio is provided, which is 1.0 times for the industry. Our company has a ratio of 0.353 times ($15,000,000 ÷ [$65,000,000 − $22,500,000]).

We would certainly wonder why we are carrying so much less in inventory than the industry. Are we doing a superior job of managing this asset, or is this an indication that we may have to forgo future sales because we do not have enough to sell? We would want to determine how aggressively we are using our suppliers to deliver materials just

---

1. From Chapter 5.

prior to the beginning of a production cycle and whether sales are being missed.

Inventory Cycle Monitoring: Metrics

Better managed companies develop internal metrics as a form of control against deterioration in financial and operating performance. Like an aging schedule (discussed in Chapter 5), these measures are used to chart the functioning of relevant activities over time. For inventory, the most important of these metrics are listed in Exhibit 6.1.

EXHIBIT 6.1

Inventory Metrics

Days in Raw Materials and WIP

Inventories of raw materials and WIP, measured in days, may show substantial variation of actual results from target (or budgeted) estimates. Trends of holding-period days for raw materials and purchased components highlight excess materials purchased, which forces the commitment of working capital. These metrics indicate the efficiency of material requirements, scheduling, and expediting (delivering inventory to required locations).

Vendor Errors

Mistakes by suppliers are usually resolved from data in purchase orders (POs) and receiving reports as matched against invoices or statements. (Purchase orders authorize vendors to ship specific items to a buying company at predetermined prices. A receiving report shows the quantity and condition of material and components as received from vendors.) However, companies typically do not keep detailed records of such errors (except as remembered "history").

It is useful to record the percentage of material shortages, overages, and below-specified quality standards by vendor, as well as the items in error, particularly as these occurrences may adversely affect production schedules or result in excess inventory. These measures can be useful in evaluating the performance of current suppliers when new POs are being negotiated.

(continued)

EXHIBIT 6.1

(continued)

Materials Movement Time

The period required to move materials to production is an important manufacturing metric when measured over time. Any deterioration in this metric should be investigated to determine whether there are vertical or horizontal movement obstacles that can delay production scheduling, or whether problems exist in developing or delivering instructions for pulling material from storage. (Vertical movement refers to multistory factories, requiring freight elevators or gravity movement. Horizontal movement involves delivery of inventory across a level platform, although problems can arise when significant distances are involved.)

Commodity Analysis

The cost of many raw materials used in a production cycle can be hedged using publicly traded commodities futures contracts or options. A useful measure in determining price volatility is the ratio of the expected purchase price to the actual purchase price plotted over time. The hedging utilization metric tracks the percentage of purchases hedged compared to total purchased dollars. Materials that cannot be protected by hedging contracts may be managed by long-term contracts with pricing guarantees.

Completion of Purchasing Cycle

The completion of the purchase order/receiver file is an important element in the management of inventory. Many companies permit the bypassing of established purchasing procedures. A particular problem is failure to follow PO requirements or to prepare receiving reports prior to authorizing payments to vendors. This metric determines the percentage of complete files for purchases that require these documents.

Damage in Movement

Inventory can be damaged in movement at any point in the manufacturing process. Careful handling is essential to minimize destruction, rework, and scrap. Metrics should be maintained on such damage to determine whether adequate care is being exercised. Such measures include percentage of materials damaged prior to production; number of rework orders compared to production orders; and percentage of materials scrapped compared to the percentage entered into production.

Assembly Line or Machinery Downtime
Production downtime may result from scheduled maintenance, staffing adjustments, insufficient materials or WIP, machinery repairs, or other causes. It is important to chart the percentage of downtime to total manufacturing time to determine trends and investigate the cause of any deterioration.

Purchasing

As we noted in our introduction to this chapter, traditional inventory management is controlled by two sets of staff: production managers, who focus on securing the necessary materials and components to manufacture goods that can be sold, and purchasing managers, who search for the lowest-cost, highest-quality supplies and equipment. Sounds logical, but who is watching your working capital? The cost of funds is seldom considered when these decisions are made, and few financial managers have ever really reviewed the processes used or the decision rules followed. Staff organizations (e.g., finance, accounting, personnel, law, and information technology) almost always defer to line organizations (sales and manufacturing) in these types of decisions.

Purchasing Cycle

Despite years of e-commerce and its predecessor, electronic data interchange (EDI), there continues to be a significant extent of manual activity in purchasing: finding vendors, issuing requests for bids, preparing purchase orders (POs), sending POs, awaiting delivery of materials, preparing reports on items delivered and any defects or shortages (receiving reports), awaiting invoices or statements, matching the PO to the receiver and to the bill, reviewing budget codes for payment authorization, preparing vouchers approving payment, and disbursing funds. If you pay by check, you have to reconcile your bank balances and fund the clearing debit.

Whew! It's no wonder that careful analysis of a single purchasing cycle takes weeks, costs $50 to $75 per PO (according to various studies), and appears to be beyond fixing. Assume that you are a large company with significant buying needs, perhaps $200 million a year. If each purchase averages $20,000, your company has 10,000 purchasing cycles a year costing about $650,000! Even if you have repetitive purchases within a single PO, the cost can still be hundreds of thousands of dollars.

Purchasing Cycle Problems

In this cycle, can any element go wrong? Here are some of the problems we've seen at companies:

- High vendor prices and too much expended on inventory. There are various sources of these situations:
  - Suppliers could simply be charging too much. This could be due to sweetheart arrangements between the vendor and your managers, or because services have not been recently rebid to more competitive vendors.
  - Local buying, often permitted to empower branch managers, to meet unexpected needs, and to maintain goodwill with the local business community. A centralized purchasing function may be perceived as unresponsive and bureaucratic, and local purchasing managers may be rewarded with lunches, golf games, and baseball tickets.

    For an example of local buying practices, see *In the Real World: Decentralized Purchasing Issues*.
  - Your processes are inefficient. You may be using production techniques that have not been reengineered or reconfigured.

Decentralized Purchasing Issues

The CFO of a large manufacturing company discovered that parts were being purchased in anticipation of pricing increases or shortages. This problem surfaced when metrics were developed on materials utilization that showed a significant increase in the days of materials held in inventory. The first step in this effort was to analyze the company's purchasing activities, which were managed at each manufacturing site. Vendor selection was made by the local production managers with advice from his or her supervisors. Maintenance of local vendor relations was considered important to ensure delivery of critical supplies.

The CFO's analysis did note that several appointments with local production decision makers were postponed due to vendor lunches and golf games. The CFO requested that any available data on prices paid for the various items purchased be forwarded to his office. However, none of the sites maintained such data, and no statistics could be provided on competitive bids, quantities purchased, pricing discounts, or net prices paid.

As a result, it was decided to pull vendor invoices for a four-month period on 40 significant inventory items, a portion of which appears below. It was discovered that the average price paid was substantially above fair market and that the range of prices was significant. It became quite obvious that local purchasing was redundant, inefficient, and expensive, and that favored vendors regularly entertained the purchasing managers.

Selected Materials Purchasing Activity

Material	Unit	Fair Market Price	Average Price Paid	Number of Purchases
Steel rods	ton	$100	$140	50
Steel sheets	unit	$ 4	$ 6	700
Pig iron	ton	$ 70	$ 85	100
Exotic metals	ounce	$700	$850	85
Lumber	1,000 board feet	$300	$400	60

Making products the same way you did in 1980 may be forcing your company to spend too much.

- You are subject to swings in the price of materials. Certain purchases are traded as commodities futures contracts, and it is possible to hedge—a form of risk management—by buying these contracts to lock in a price for later delivery.[2] *Futures* are derivative contracts that give the buyer the right but not the obligation to buy or sell specified amounts of commodities, interest rates, and other physical or financial assets.

For example, farmers use futures to be guaranteed a price when their produce goes to market, perhaps six months or more after planting. By selling a futures contract in March for delivery in October, they know that adequate revenue will be received at harvest to cover the costs of labor, seed, equipment, and energy, in addition to other expenses. Buyers of futures contracts include speculators and actual users of the asset (such as baking companies for wheat and airlines for gasoline).

The extra cost of this behavior has been variously estimated at 15 to 25 percent through higher prices, lower order quantity, and tacit acceptance of lessened quality. Reducing or better management of local purchasing can improve the forecasting of future requirements and the determination of economic order quantity (to be discussed later).

---

2. A *hedge* is a position established in one market in an attempt to offset exposure to price fluctuations in an opposite position with the goal of minimizing exposure to unwanted risk.

- POs and receiving reports may not be issued. In our experience, about one-fourth of all buying does not conform to these procedures. If there is no PO, unauthorized company employees can make and approve a purchase. If there is no receiver, defects and missing items may be overlooked. Purchasing that follows established rules usually occurs with essential, repetitive buys, such as raw materials, paper, shipping materials, and office supplies. The process is most often incomplete for technical or specialized products, such as technology and engineering instruments. Without proper documentation, you might as well hand over your company's checkbook to your vendors!

- Bills may not be reviewed for authorization or matched to POs and receivers. The accounts payables department receives an invoice or a statement and verifies that appropriate approvals have been attached. But where are the PO and/or the receiver? We'll discuss payables in Chapter 7; for the present discussion, note that most payables functions go ahead and pay the vendor even if the PO and/or receiver is missing.

Review *Tips and Techniques: Investigating Your Payables History* for ideas on analyzing your payables practices.

TIPS AND TECHNIQUES

Investigating Your Payables History

Hire temps (perhaps college students) to pull three months of paid invoices from the home and branch offices. Have the following data logged onto a spreadsheet:

- Dollar amount
- Whether the cash discount was taken
- Invoice date and date of payment

EOQ and JIT

Supply chain management (SCM) attempts to optimize all of the components of a manufacturing process, including purchasing, inventory management, and transportation logistics.[3] Two key concepts in SCM are economic order quantity (EOQ) and just-in-time (JIT).

Economic Order Quantity

Economic order quantity (EOQ) is a mathematical model that calculates the optimal size of materials or components purchases. It is also used in

---

3. Numerous excellent SCM references are available, including Michael H. Hugos, *Essentials of Supply Chain Management, 2nd edition* (Hoboken, NJ: John Wiley & Sons, Inc., 2006); and Thomas Schoenfeldt, *A Practical Application of Supply Chain Management Principles* (Milwaukee, IL: ASQ Quality Press, 2008).

making production lot size decisions. Buying decisions may fail to consider the cost of carrying inventory, the real value of volume discounts offered, or the potential loss from stale inventory. For example, one large manufacturing company frequently acquired materials and components far in advance of the start of their production cycle, resulting in excessive carrying costs and some unusable materials due to changes in production requirements and natural inventory decay.

The average holding period for this company was 70 days, which reduced the realized gross margin (sales − cost of goods sold) by 1.5 percent, from 10 percent to 8.5 percent. The impact on the company's return on equity (ROE) was 2 percent, with the target ROE of 16 percent declining to 14 percent.[4] The role of finance in this situation is to determine the EOQ, calculate the value and costs of volume discounts based on recent experience, and support decisions that optimize results.

Calculation of EOQ

The optimal order quantity can be determined from the following calculation:

$$Q^* = \sqrt{\frac{2TF}{CC}}$$

where $Q^* = \text{EOQ}$
$T = \text{total sales in units}$
$F = \text{fixed purchase order (PO) cost}$
$CC = \text{carrying cost of inventory per unit}$

Assume that we expect 5,000 units in sales, a purchase order cost of $50, a price per unit of $10, and a carrying cost per unit of $1. (*Carrying cost* is the cost of holding inventory, and includes warehousing costs such

---

4. For a discussion of the methodology used in these calculations, see James Sagner, *Financial and Process Metrics for the New Economy* (New York: AMACOM, 2001).

as rent, utilities and salaries, financial costs and inventory costs related to perishability, shrinkage, and insurance). The resulting EOQ is calculated as about 700 units, with an average inventory on hand of 350 units (or one-half). Few companies actually do these calculations, and, in fact, do not know their PO cost or the carrying cost of inventory. Instead, orders are either based on sales forecasts, which are usually optimistic, or the inventory carried is minimized, following the Japanese concept of just-in-time.

Just-In-Time

Just-in-time (JIT) attempts to set the minimum required inventory of materials through careful planning and management of production cycles. JIT means having the right materials, parts, and products in the right place at the right time, on the theory that excess inventory means waste and cost. Successful JIT programs rely on the ability of vendors to meet tight delivery schedules and a high level of quality control.

However, if a disaster affects a vendor, such as a weather situation or a fire, your business activities may be adversely affected. Even a delay in transporting materials, a frequent event in winter months, can be a problem. In the current credit crisis, companies fail and your JIT supplier may be forced into bankruptcy. In that situation, the economics of JIT may look fairly insignificant when you have no materials or components for your production line.

Work in Process

As noted at the start of this chapter, the work-in-process (WIP) cycle involves the second component of inventory and includes the management of materials and components as they are retrieved and used to produce goods for sale. From an accounting perspective, the costing of WIP requires an inspection of inventory as it progresses through a manufacturing cycle and an estimate of the approximate stage (or percent) of completion.

WIP Cycle Management

It is important to analyze WIP because of the inherent inefficiencies in many manufacturing situations. According to various observers, only a small portion of manufacturing cycle time is actually spent in the production of a good, with considerable delays for queuing, inspection, physical movement to the next production activity, temporary packaging and storage, and similar activities.[5] These delays are aggravated by changes due to customer requirements, engineering specifications, order quantities, and manufacturing processes.

Long WIP cycles contribute to rigidity in manufacturing and reduce a company's flexibility to alter production routines to meet nonstandard customer demands. While consumer products are usually not subject to unusual requirements, large systems and some business products nearly always have a particular configuration. This problem indirectly affects a company's capability to respond to the pressure from global competitors and likely raises delivered prices.

In most companies, it is extremely costly to institute a manufacturing change. The strategy traditionally considered to be the most economical is mass production and long production runs. As an alternative approach, some producers acquire equipment that can produce different products by simply changing fabrication tools and manufacturing configurations. The strategy should be to foster flexible and customized production with decentralized control, with the goals of reducing setup time and smoothing the production schedule on the basis of customer demands. See the *In the Real World: Benefits of Supply Chain Management* example for a solution developed by a consumer electronics company.

---

5. According to Brian H. Maskell, less than 5 percent of production time is actually used for manufacturing activities. See *Performance Measurement for World Class Manufacturing* (Portland, OR: Productivity Press, 1991), p. 124.

Benefits of Supply Chain Management

A manufacturer of consumer electrics confronted variations in demand and inefficiencies in supply chain management (SCM) that strained resources, delayed time-to-market and increased supply chain costs. The company decided to outsource to a SCM software vendor (see the list in Exhibit 6.3) enabling the focus of its scarce internal resources on furthering its core competencies of research and the development of innovative products. Several elements were required for a workable solution:

- Implementation of a flexible supply chain capable of meeting peak demand spikes without service disruption or other delays.

- Initiation of efficient logistics programs to improve repair cycle times and customer satisfaction.

- Creation of an infrastructure that accommodates anticipated distributor and consumer sales growth of more than 300 percent in the next two years with minimal risk and capital expenditure by the company.

Results included the following:

- Improvement in production efficiencies with close to 100 percent of orders shipped on time to end users.

- Consistent achievement of 99 percent order accuracy.

- Reduction in sales returns program cycle time, achieving a 36-hour turnaround, thereby strengthening customer loyalty.

- Improvement in customer service by maintaining high service levels during peak demand cycles where demand increases from an average of 30,000 products to more than 80,000 in a single month.

- Reduction in the time required to bring products to market, improving efficiency and reducing total costs.

Supply Chain Management Systems

The impact of global competition has forced companies to deemphasize the management of physical inventory and to focus on information about the supply chain. This problem is compounded when there are hundreds of items in various locations organized by different identifiers, such as serial numbers, container or bin numbers, and unique product codes. Various SCM systems have been developed to integrate data on inventory quantity, location, status of WIP, expectation of delivery from suppliers, promises of delivery to customers, costs incurred, likely sales price, forecasting of future demand, and other functions. See Exhibit 6.2 for a representative listing of SCM capabilities.

EXHIBIT 6.2

Typical SCM Functions

Inventory Management

- Inventory manifest preparation
- Order alert and target stock levels for multiple warehouses
- Reporting for items below reorder alert levels and target stock levels
- Lot and serial numbers assignment to inventory
- Inbound stock reservation for customer back orders
- Assignment and stock transfer of inventory to multiple warehouses
- Inventory tracking in multiple picking locations
- Inventory valuation reports by alternative costing methods (e.g., FIFO, LIFO, average cost)
- Order management modules

Order Management

- Inventory information during order entry
- Estimated time of arrival for inbound vendor orders
- Order status by due date
- Notification to customers on order status
- Billing and shipping addresses editing during order entry
- Customer payment information

(continued)

EXHIBIT 6.2

(continued)

- Bill of lading and packing slip printing
- Integration with common carriers (e.g., FedEx, UPS, USPS)
- Assign freight to calculate landed costs

Manufacturing

- Bill of materials tracking
- Work order item assemblies
- Customized item assemblies work orders
- Reporting of material requirements and cost tracking

The complexity of this analyses forces companies to use SCM systems provided by specialized software vendors. The demand for these products has created a $7 billion a year business, with leading vendors of these systems including SAP, Oracle/JD Edwards, and JDA Software.[6] For a listing, see Exhibit 6.3. There are versions of these systems now available for nearly any size company. Although specific quantitative

EXHIBIT 6.3

SCM Software Vendors

Rank	Company Name	2009 Revenue	Web Site
1	SAP	$942 million	www.sap.com
2	Oracle	$715 million	www.oracle.com
3	JDA Software	$390 million	www.jda.com
4	Manhattan Associates	$337 million	www.manh.com
5	RedPrairie	$293 million	www.redprairie.com
6	i2 Technologies	$255 million	www.i2.com
7	Infor	$177 million	www.infor.com
8	ILOG	$175 million	www.ilog.com
9	IBS	$171 million	www.ibsus.com
10	Epicor	$138 million	www.epicor.com

6. Bob Trebilcock and Lorie King Rogers, "2009: Top 20 Supply Chain Management Software Suppliers," *Modern Materials Handling* (www.mmh.com), July 1, 2009, reporting on research by AMR Research.

savings vary, reported benefits include reductions in working capital requirements, increased customer satisfaction, and improved integration with corporate strategic initiatives.

Asset-Based Financing: Inventory

Asset-based financing (ABF), discussed in Chapter 5 regarding accounts receivable, is used for working capital with a company's inventory functioning as the collateral for the loan. Lenders typically use a conservative valuation of inventory and make loans for somewhat less than the valuation figure, with the key factor being marketability of that collateral. Typical lender discounting allows a loan of 60 to 80 percent of the value of a retail inventory. A manufacturer's inventory, consisting of parts and other unfinished materials, might be only 40 percent of value. Interest rates charged on inventory financing are similar to those for receivables lending. The interest cost is usually the prime rate plus about 2 percent.

Inventory that is financed through ABF programs typically are industrial and consumer durables that can be readily identified by serial number or other tag. Some lenders specialize by line of business. For example, Textron Financial lends to aviation and golf course customers, while ORIX lends on technology purchases. Selected industries that could consider ABF are noted in Exhibit 6.4.

Asset-Based Lenders: Inventory

Selected inventory lenders include:

- Bank of America
- CIT Group
- Citigroup
- GE Commercial Finance
- ORIX Corporation
- Textron Financial
- Wells Fargo

EXHIBIT 6.4

Industries That Use Inventory as Collateral in ABF

Agricultural equipment

Electronics and appliances

Food service and equipment

Home furnishings

Hearth

HVAC (heating, ventilating, and air conditioning) equipment

Lawn and garden

Manufactured housing

Marine industry

Motorsport vehicles and equipment

Musical instruments

Office products

Pool and spa

Recreational vehicles

Sewing and vacuum

Technology products

Trailers

Working with ABF lenders that accept inventory as collateral requires different skills from borrowing from a bank through a line of credit. See *Tips and Techniques: ABL Using Inventory* for specific ideas.

TIPS AND TECHNIQUES

ABL Using Inventory

Companies considering using inventory as collateral in an arrangement with an asset-based lender should consider the following:

- Typically your business is experiencing rapid growth—highly leveraged and undercapitalized.

- Your inventory turns several times a year and there is some seasonality.
- Borrowing requirements are substantial (above $500,000) to justify the lender's cost to monitor the loan.
- A good inventory tracking system is required with tags, labels, bar codes, or other unique identifiers.
- Daily communications with your lender on the sale of specific inventory items.
- Deposits of collections into a bank account designated by your lender.
- Use of other banking services of the lender if available; i.e., for disbursements to other vendors and for payroll.
- Strict loan covenants limits on other borrowing arrangements, and on the payment of salaries and dividends.
- Periodic visits by the lender to ascertain adherence to the loan agreement.
- Lender expectation that stale inventory will be periodically purged.

These restrictions may be onerous, so any ABF decision should be carefully considered.

Summary

The two aspects of inventory management are the purchasing of materials and components and the management of those materials and components as they are retrieved and used to produce goods for sale ("work in process"). Several economic and financial factors are relevant in managing inventory, including price, volume purchasing, pricing concessions, and the timing of delivery of material prior to the beginning of manufacturing. The integration of these concepts through supply chain management involves economic order quantity and just-in-time. As with receivables, asset-based financing using inventory has become an important source of working capital credit.

CHAPTER 7

Payables and Working Capital Issues

After reading this chapter, you will be able to:

- Consider appropriate policies and organization for payables management.
- Understand how ratios and other metrics assist in payables management.
- Learn about active versus passive management of payables.
- Evaluate internal processes and outsourcing alternatives in managing payables.
- Review methods of disbursing payroll including direct deposit and paycards.

The current liability with the most working capital significance is accounts payable, which involves payments to vendors for inventory, supplies, and services. There can be little dispute as to the need to pay bills as they become due. However, decisions on payment dates and practices is often turned over to payables clerks who have limited knowledge of the float consequences of their actions. As a result, companies make poor choices on when to pay, whether to take cash discounts, and how to manage the payables portion of the cash-flow timeline. In addition, current liabilities involve the payment of salaries and wages; techniques for managing this activity are included in this chapter.

Elements of Payables Management

There are important elements in establishing a program to manage payables, including establishing policies, organizing for policy implementation, and monitoring results.

Developing Payables Policies

Policies formalize decisions on the decision to disburse company funds for payables. In addition to the inventory rules listed in Chapter 6, decisions should be thoughtfully considered on several issues, including the following:

- Should we pay our vendors on or after established terms; for example, if the terms are net 30, should we pay on day 30 or a specified number of days after day 30 (which is the practice in many companies)?

- If cash discounts are offered, should we take the discount?

- Should we demand prorated discounts ("dynamic discounting") for any payment made before the net period ends?

- How should we handle situations when documentation is missing from a bill, such as a PO, a receiving report, an authorization (whether by signature or voucher), and/or budget codes?

- If a vendor requests special treatment (such as an occasional early payment), should we comply?

- Should we allow vendors to buy lunches, drinks, or similar entertainment for our payables staff? If this is allowed, what limits are appropriate?

- Should we operate our own payables cycle or should we outsource payment activities to a bank or other provider?

Policies establish required practice for all parties that cannot be modified except by senior management. This is important when payables clerks are approached by vendor representatives with early payment requests or offers of entertainment. Any violation should trigger appropriate responses by management.

Organizing for Payables Management

Many companies have an accounts payable manager responsible for the payment of bills from vendors. There are large float and cost implications of payables, and inappropriate decisions or inefficient procedures can add significant costs, adversely impacting working capital. Because of these considerations, the payables manager should meet frequently with finance and other relevant functions.

Payables Cycle Monitoring: Ratios

We calculated various working capital ratios in Chapter 1; however, there is no standard accounts payable ratio. RMA (the Risk Management Association) publishes supplemental ratios including payables turnover, defined as cost of goods sold ("cost of sales") divided by payables. For plastics manufacturing, the result is 21, 11, and 8 turns, and 17, 32, and 47 days. The Rengas Company has $100 million in cost of goods sold and $15 million in payables, resulting in 6.7 turns and 54 days.

These results are slightly above the interquartile range, meaning that any lengthening of the payables cycle—that is, paying more slowly— would likely impair vendor relationships. The common-size balance sheet data we noted in the previous chapter can also be used to analyze payables. Our company had 12 percent (of total liabilities and net worth) in payables, while the industry results showed 16.2 percent. This is not a significant variation from the industry.

Payables Metrics

Various metrics can be used to measure a company's performance in managing payables.

- *Issuance of accounts payable disbursements.* Payables practice may be at variance with predetermined target dates. Such targets can be the discount date, the due date, or an established number of days after the due date. It is useful to determine industry practice by reference to industry ratios or statistics provided by trade associations, or at least to establish the parameters for payment so that the decision is not left to the discretion of payables clerks. For example, if our competitors pay an average of ten days after the due date, when should we pay?

- *Cash discounts taken/not taken.* Although only about 10 percent of vendors offer discounts, any such opportunities should be individually evaluated and either explicitly taken or passed. Many companies either take all or none of the discounts offered, which is suboptimal practice. In addition, it may be possible to negotiate "dynamic discounting" with vendors offering prorated discounts based on days paid prior to the due date.

- *Use of bank disbursement products.* While many companies prefer to use check disbursement systems to pay vendors to either extend float or have a paper trail proving the payment, there are attractive and cost effective bank products that should be considered. A metric logging the review and use of these alternatives to traditional disbursing should be developed.

- *Positive pay and account reconciliation.* Certain bank services are primarily used for control to assure that payments are not altered and fraudulently diverted.[1] Logs should be maintained to indicate company compliance with appropriate audit controls.

1. See Chapter 2.

Accounts Payable Function

Although accounts payable in the typical company is not accorded much visibility, the tasks performed are vital: reviewing POs and receiving reports against bills from vendors, finding discrepancies, approving or requesting clarification or additional documentation, and requesting that disbursements be issued. The actual check printing and mailing function is often split between finance, information technology (to actually print the checks and remittance advices[2]), and the mailroom.

Active versus Passive Payables Management

A company may not attempt to actively manage the payables function and merely pay bills as presented if the necessary authorizations and accounting codes are provided and supporting documentation is attached. In these situations, there is little concern for the appropriateness of the expense, for the value of float, or for variances among vendors as to their need for timely payment. In fact, a vendor payment may be made before the due date if a formal "diarying" system does not exist. Each vendor must be individually examined to determine optimal practice. For an illustration of poor practices, see *In the Real World: Float Costs of Mismanaged Payables*.

IN THE REAL WORLD

Float Costs of Mismanaged Payables

The business of the World of Animals is to stock zoos. Working capital was a continuing problem, and a study of payable practices seemed appropriate. Disbursements were made by check,

---

2. A *remittance advice* is normally attached to a check indicating which bills are being paid and whether items are in dispute.

with two major payables runs on the 5th and 20th of each month. The results for its largest vendors are displayed below, showing an annual value of float costing nearly $30,000.

World of Animals: Billing Activity of Largest Vendors (All invoices are received on the first or second of the month)

Vendor and Accompanying Note	Terms	Usual Payment Date	Days Paid Early vs. Net Terms	Discounts Offered	Amount of Annual Purchases (most recent year)	Value of Foregone Float (at 10%)
Amy's Alligators (1)	1/10, n/30	5th	25	1/10 discount	$3,800,000	N/A
Ben's Bobcats (2)	net 20	20th	0		$2,200,000	$ 0
Charlie's Cassowaries (3)	net 30	20th	10		$2,000,000	$ 5,550
Claire's Cobras (4)	net 30	20th	10		$1,500,000	$ 4,170
Denali's Deer (5)	2/10, n/30	5th		2/10 discount	$ 925,000	N/A
Owen's Ostriches (6)	net 30	20th	10		$ 830,000	$ 2,300
Robert-Paul's Ravens (7)	2/20, n/90	20th	70	2/20 discount	$ 740,000	$14,390
Sarah's Sea Lions (8)	net 30	5th	25		$ 635,000	$ 880
Stephen's Scorpions (9)	1/20, n/30	20th	10	1/20 discount	$ 700,000	N/A
Tessa's Tigers (10)	net 45	5th	10*		$ 670,000	$ 1,860
Annual Cost of Float Foregone						$29,150

*Paid on 5th of the second month with the final due date of the 15th of that month.
N/A = not applicable

Notes:
1. Amy's cash discount was valued at 18% (30 − 10 = 20; 360 ÷ 20 = 18 × 1%) and worth taking.
2. Ben's was paid on the due date.
3. Charlie's was paid 10 days early, valued as ($2 million ÷ 360 × 10 × 10%).
4. Claire's was paid 10 days early, valued as ($1.5 million ÷ 360 × 10 × 10%).
5. Denali's cash discount was valued at 36% (30 − 10 = 20; 360 ÷ 20 = 18 × 2%) and worth taking.
6. Owen's was paid 10 days early, valued as ($830,000 ÷ 360 × 10 × 10%).
7. Robert-Paul's was paid 70 days early versus the due date, valued as ($740,000 ÷ 360 × 70 × 10%). The cash discount was valued as 10.3% (90 − 20 = 70; 360 ÷ 70 = 5.15 × 2 = 10.3%), and not worth taking.
8. Sarah's was paid 5 days early, valued as ($635,000 ÷ 360 × 5 × 10%).
9. Stephen's cash discount was valued at 36% (30 − 20 = 10; 360 ÷ 10 = 36 × 1%) and worth taking.
10. Tessa's was paid 10 days early, valued as ($670,000 ÷ 360 × 10 × 10%).

Other companies actively manage payables to maximize float while maintaining good vendor relations. Decisions are made regarding the importance of each supplier, and markers in the payables system indicate whether cash discounts should be taken or if an invoice should be paid on or after the due date. These "pay fast/pay slow" alternatives require accounts payable managers to emerge from their clerical function of paying invoices as presented, to manage the process against such constraints as vendor sensitivity and the time value of money.

Regardless of the approach chosen by companies in managing payables, many now use integrated purchasing/payables systems. These products offer various analytics, including controls on purchasing and payment decisions, limits on access to lists of approved vendors, file maintenance of all relevant vendor data, and interfaces with disbursement systems. Later generations of purchasing/payables, known as enterprise resource planning systems (ERP), are integrated with various business applications.[3] We'll discuss ERP systems in Chapter 9.

---

3. ERP is an integrated system that manages internal and external resources of a company including tangible assets, financial resources, and materials purchasing. ERP systems are based on a centralized computing platform, consolidating all significant business operations into a uniform environment. The vendors of SCM software in Exhibit 6.3 also provide ERP systems.

Payables Using Internal Processes

Businesses that complete the payables cycle through company functions have the option of disbursing using checks, ACH or Fedwire, or through procurement cards. In these situations, the entire process is handled internally although banks allow companies to stop disputed payments before the transaction is complete.

Checks, ACH, and Fedwire

Checks, ACH, and Fedwire (previously discussed in Chapter 2) are the most usual methods of disbursement for payables. A regular bank checking account receives activity during normal business hours, which means that any holder of a check can request funds from the account (or "cash" the check) at any time. The account owner must either leave balances or transfer funds into the account to cover such activity, or risk the embarrassment and expense of checks returned to depositors (your vendors) for nonsufficient funds (NSF).

A better alternative is a controlled disbursement account, which is funded once during the business day to cover daily check presentments, eliminating the need for companies to leave balances to cover clearing items. Early notification of that day's clearings allows funding of the account and helps the finance manager determine the company's cash position. The funding is by intrabank transfer, through an interbank ACH or by Fedwire.

The company completes the payables activity by releasing the payment in satisfaction of an outstanding invoice. However, the bank will require resolution of any mismatches of issued file data compared to clearing data if positive pay is used. If the payment is by ACH, the rules of the clearinghouse (NACHA) require that a prenotification ACH be satisfactorily completed before the ACH can be completed. Due to their cost, Fedwires are infrequently used for disbursements and are final once released.

Procurement Cards

Procurement cards (also known as purchasing cards) are corporate cards issued to designated employees to make local purchases on behalf of the company. These cards differ from credit cards in the following respects:

- The company (rather than the employee) receives the bill and is responsible for payment.

- Codes are imbedded in the card to restrict purchases to eligible types of products and services and to limit the total amount spent.

- Automated data capture enables the company to receive next-day summaries of purchasing activities for company review and the determination of appropriateness and accuracy.

Purchasing can be simplified through the use of the cards for routine items. A major procurement card benefit is the elimination of the paperwork inherent in creating a PO and other documentation. In addition, volume discounts may be arranged with frequently used vendors, and employees can be encouraged or instructed to use those suppliers.

Savings arising from procurement card programs can be 80 to 90 percent of the cost of the traditional PO cycle. Opposition to card programs has been primarily from purchasing departments who see these cards as a threat to their position in the company. However, widespread card usage has minimized this problem, particularly as management is generally pleased with the savings typically achieved. Furthermore, the use of cards for small items allows purchasing managers to concentrate on major buying decisions and to negotiate with vendors for volume discounts when cards are presented. Nearly every large and regional bank now has a procurement card program.

Payables Outsourcing

The outsourcing of various payables flows may be effective strategies for companies.

Freight Bills

There are numerous organizations that offer comprehensive freight and logistics services, including the auditing and payment of bills from transportation carriers.[4] Freight invoices are reviewed for excessive charges such as misclassifications, incorrect discount levels, incorrect mileage calculations, extension mistakes, and other errors. Overcharge claims can be filed and tracked to request refunds of fees overpaid.

Other services offered include verification of shipper liability, rate negotiation, review of contracts, classification and routing assistance, customized transportation and distribution systems, carrier selection, and contract negotiations. These freight payment services audit both large freight movements and small parcel services such as UPS, FedEx, and DHL. A particular concern is on-time performance and the filing of claims for refunds if delivery does not occur within the time guarantee.

Here's the typical data flow: Based on your instructions, your carriers submit freight invoices to your freight payment provider. The firm will verify the freight movement by reviewing bills of lading[5] and signed proof of delivery, and accuracy of the invoice will be determined by examination of freight rates, freight discounts, misapplied charges, and other sources of potential errors. In addition, recommendations are made regarding the use of carriers, transportation and logistics systems, packaging and container labels, and payment alternatives.

Comprehensive Payables Concepts

Several banks offer a complete disbursement outsourcing service generically referred to as *comprehensive payables*. The company authorizing

---

4. See, for example, www.cassinfo.com, which is the web site of Cass Information Systems. Other prominent global companies include C. H. Robinson Worldwide, www.chrobinson.com; CEVA Group Plc, www.cevalogistics.com; and DB Schenker, www.dbschenker.com.
5. A *bill of lading* is a document issued by a carrier to a shipping company that specified goods have been received on board as cargo for transporting to a named place to a recipient (usually the purchaser).

payments transmits a file in any of several formats containing the follow-ing payment data:

- Due date of payment (as payments can be warehoused by the bank).

- Dollar amount.

- Payee and payee's address.

- Mechanism; i.e., check, Fedwire, or ACH.

- Accompanying remittance detail.

The bank creates payments as instructed and issues them on a speci-fied date. Some banks determine the appropriate payment mechanism based on company-determined parameters. Electronic payments are issued as requested by the company, and transaction fees are based on the bank's standard pricing.

Check Payments in a Comprehensive Payables Environment

When a check is the preferred method of payment, the disbursement is prepared for mailing including any desired remittance detail. Data provided typically includes invoice or item numbers being paid and adjustments to the invoiced amount, including discounts taken or credits for damaged merchandise. Certain industries require lengthy descrip-tions of payments, such as the explanation-of-benefits (EOB) statements provided by insurance companies to insured individuals and healthcare providers.

Most comprehensive payables banks can process all of these activi-ties, including stuffing envelopes and applying postage. Banks can also print company logos, signature lines, and promotional statements, such as "Ask us about direct deposit." Inexpensive desktop technology allows the issuance of emergency checks and the transmission of a supplemental issued file to the bank.

The bank will attempt to gain the highest postal discount offered by the USPS for quantity mailings. The amount of the discount varies by the quantity of items to each receiving zip code and other criteria.[6] As the checks clear, the bank performs the usual positive pay service, and funds the resulting daily debit based on instructions from the company. In addition, account reconciliation and check storage are provided. *Tips and Techniques: Costs of Check Issuance* discusses issues in calculating your disbursement expenses.

Benefits of Comprehensive Payables

There are significant benefits to companies using comprehensive payables.

- Consolidation of the payments function. Instead of having to maintain different systems for various types of payments, companies can use a single system for all disbursements.

- Outsourcing the entire disbursement function including check printing, mailing, and the reconciliation process. Several internal company responsibilities can be entirely eliminated, and the risk of

TIPS AND TECHNIQUES

Costs of Check Issuance

Companies that issue disbursements for payables should carefully examine the all-in cost, not just the bank check clearing charge. The table below lists a company's charges for 3,000 vendor checks a month, with the cost of nearly $7 per payment totaling almost $250,000 a year. Using another disbursement method would result in significant savings. Per item bank charges range from about $0.10 for ACH to about $0.75 for comprehensive payables. If the latter were used, avoidable costs are about two-thirds of the charges in *italics* and all of the charges in CAPITAL LETTERS. The potential savings are some $140,000 ($247,500 – $108,967).

6. For further information see bulkmail.info/fcrates.html or www.usps.gov.

Labor	Hours Per Month	Cost Per Hour	Current Monthly Cost	Comprehensive Payables Alternative Proposed Monthly Cost
Computer processing	50	$50	$ 2,500	$ 833
COMPUTER PRINTER	30	$40	$ 1,200	$ 0
BURSTING AND SIGNING	30	$20	$ 600	$ 0
Disbursement management	30	$30	$ 900	$ 900
FOLDING AND STUFFING	75	$20	$ 1,500	$ 0
MAIL OPERATIONS	15	$20	$ 300	$ 0
RECONCILIATION	20	$30	$ 600	$ 0
Report preparation	10	$35	$ 350	$ 117
Total labor			$ 7,950	$ 1,849

Supplies and Banking	Volume Per Month	Cost Per Item	Current Monthly Cost	Proposed Monthly Cost
CHECK STOCK	3,000	$0.05	$ 150	$ 0
REMITTANCE ADVICES	3,000	$0.10	$ 300	$ 0
ENVELOPES	3,000	$0.05	$ 150	$ 0
PRINTER SUPPLIES			$ 75	$ 0
BANK CHARGES (all services)	3,000	$0.50	$ 1,500	$ 0
Postage	3,000	$0.45	$ 1,350	$ 1,350
Total materials			$ 3,525	$ 1,350

Fixed Costs	Equipment Used	Cost of Equipment	Monthly Cost	Proposed Monthly Cost
PRINTER	3	$350	$ 1,050	$ 0
FOLDING AND STUFFING EQUIPMENT	2	$300	$ 600	$ 0
Software support			$ 2,000	$ 666
POSTAGE METERS	2	$100	$ 200	$ 0
Computer			$ 2,000	$ 666
Rent allocation			$ 1,500	$ 500
Senior management			$ 1,800	$ 1,800
Total fixed costs			$ 9,150	$ 3,632
Total Monthly Costs			$ 20,625	$ 6,831
Total Annual Costs			$247,500	$ 81,972
Cost per Disbursement			$ 6.875	$ 2.277

Annual Costs of Comprehensive Payables		
Disbursement Costs	$247,500	$ 81,967
Banking Costs		$ 27,000
Total Costs		$108,967

internal fraud is significantly diminished with the process managed by a bank.[7]

- Cost savings. Studies indicate that the all-in cost of creating and sending a payment is approximately $5.00, although fees vary by issuer. Banks are currently bidding the service for about $0.75 for paper disbursements. Electronic disbursements are charged at the bank's price for ACH or Fedwire, with an additional charge for managing the disbursement process. The company continues to have some expenses for general bank contact, including overall supervision and the daily "pay" or "no pay" positive pay decision. A rough estimate of the total cost of using a bank for outsourced payments is $1 per transaction plus postage.

- Vendor access to payment status. As the process is on a hosted web-based platform, vendors can log onto the system at any time and view the status of their invoices and payments pending. Some banks (e.g., Bank of America) allow vendors to factor these receivables to accelerate cash flow.

Paying electrically through the ACH can develop significant savings; for one organization's experience, see *In the Real World: Electronic Disbursements*.

Payroll Alternatives

ACH direct deposit is the principal method now used by companies for payroll, although checks are still issued when requested by employees. The widespread acceptance of this payroll mechanism has been a fairly recent phenomenon, assisted by active promotion by banks and employers, and by the obvious advantages of convenience and day of pay access to the funds.

---

7. A chronic source of fraud is inadequately supervised blank check stock. On more than one occasion blank checks have been stolen from unlocked file drawers, issued to phony businesses, and cashed. A suggested fix is printing the entire check face on blank paper at the time that the check is prepared; for one vendor's solution, see www.troygroup.com.

IN THE REAL WORLD

Electronic Disbursements

A large hospital and medical center received a high percentage of invoices in paper form requiring extensive manual handling including validation, review, and approval. An electronic settlement process allowed the hospital to involve all of its suppliers including medical, pharmaceutical, office supplies, food service, and construction; other vendors such as legal services and printing companies were later added.

As the result, savings were developed throughout the payables cycle:

- Comprehensive payables grew to three-fourths of all disbursements.
- The cycle to complete payables was compressed from 80 to 20 days.
- Exceptions and adjustments were reduced by one-sixth.
- The percent of cash discounts increased to three times the amount offered to the typical buying company.

Mechanics of Direct Deposit

The employee provides a voided check to his or her employer at the time of employment or later enrollment. The transit routing and bank account data from the bottom of the check are used to build a file record. Depending on the arrangement with the disbursement bank, the ACH transfer is made one or two days before the pay date, assuring that good funds will be in the employee's account on the pay date. Alternatively, an outside payroll service calculates the amount of net pay, the various deductions including tax and employee-paid benefits, and transmits a file of these data to the bank that is used. The leading payroll services are ADP, Paychex, Administaff, and Trinet Group.

The primary advantages of direct deposit are:

- Low cost to the employer as the cost of an ACH is about $0.10 (versus $5.00 to issue and reconcile a payroll check).

- Reduced employee absence as there is no reason for the employee to leave company premises to deposit or cash the payroll check.

- Convenience for the employee as the pay is in the bank regardless of weather, vacation, business travel, or the loss of the payroll envelope.

- The funds are credited to the employee's account, the earnings on which, depending on the type of depository account, may or may not pay interest for his or her benefit. However, earnings on deposit accounts are fairly nominal so this should be a minor consideration.

- Fraud prevention as there is no need to verify the identification of an employee attempting to cash a payroll check.

Disadvantages include the following:

- The employer loses all use of the funds deposited for the payroll—the float—on pay date. Studies of payroll check clearings show that the average delay in check clearing is about three business days.

- The employer must manage a dual payroll system—check and direct deposit—unless all of payroll is converted to electronic. This is not a major concern for companies that use an outsource service.

For ideas on selling the electronic deposit of wages and salaries to your employees, see *Tips and Techniques: Promoting Payroll Direct Deposit.*

Paycards

Employees may choose not to receive a direct deposit or a check for various reasons. Many banks and payroll services offer paycards, which are ATM cards specifically used for payroll. The employee need not

Promoting Payroll Direct Deposit

Employees who resist direct deposit may be hiding pay from a spouse or significant other, may not have a bank account, or are simply uninformed about the mechanics of the program. Companies can require direct deposit as a condition of employment (but not after), but must allow employees to select the financial institution to which their pay is sent.

You should consider involving your bank in providing an educational program to assist in overcoming resistance. Companies find that their bank is happy to market their services to your employees, and promotions often used are a year's free checking, a discounted mortgage or home loan program, no-fee credit cards, or other promotions. The current banking environment may be an excellent time to offer these services to your employees.

Sufficient employment at your single site may justify the bank installing an ATM for employee banking (which your company may have to subsidize). Your company will benefit by eliminating petty cash maintained to accommodate check cashing and travel or expense reimbursement. In addition to the management and replenishment of these funds, the company avoids the risk of theft.

have an account at the payroll bank. Instead, an ATM card is issued along with a PIN number, allowing access through any ATM machine or at merchants that accept the card family (e.g., Visa or MasterCard). The employee receives a monthly statement detailing withdrawals, payroll credits, and purchases.

Paycard is a convenient way of paying seasonal workers and other employees who may be at a job for only a short period of time. Other employer paycard advantages include:

- Reduction or elimination of stop payment fees for lost or stolen paychecks.

- Minimizing exposure to paycheck fraud.

- Elimination of employer cashing of checks.

Advantages for employees include:

- No time wasted waiting in lines at banks or check-cashing stores.

- No fees for check cashing.

- No requirement for multiple forms of identification to cash checks.

- Access to funds anytime and virtually anywhere.

Summary

Decisions about accounts payable dates and practices are made by disbursement clerks in many companies, who have limited knowledge of the float consequences of their actions. As a result, suboptimal choices are often made on when to pay, whether to take cash discounts, and how to manage the payables portion of the cash-flow timeline. There are various processes that should be considered in disbursing funds, including the traditional mechanisms noted in Chapter 2, procurement cards, outsourcing methods such as freight and logistics services and comprehensive payables, and direct deposit and paycard for payroll.

PART III

Issues in Working Capital Management

*N**ote:* This is the conclusion of the Widget Manufacturing Case which opened Parts I and II of this book. A suggested solution is provided in Appendix A.

Comprehensive Case: Widget Manufacturing Case III

Once Arnold began to implement various working capital changes, the position of Widget Manufacturing significantly improved. In fact, I. M. Clueless (Arnold's banker) was impressed by his willingness to take the necessary steps to collect overdue receivables and sell excess inventory, and responded by extending the company's credit line. There was even consideration of a new production site (see Part II of the case), but the original idea of locating in the United States began to refocus on Mexico.

Mexican Option

Considering Mexico or any other international site had been totally out of Arnold's mind-set. However, as I. M. introduced Arnold to various international experts at Second National, the idea of moving into a global market began to have significant appeal. The bankers noted the extensive manufacturing experience that several Mexican companies had in consumer electronics, the significantly lower labor cost, the incentives provided by the Mexican government for new businesses, free trade between NAFTA countries, and the potential gateway to Latin American retailers and their customers.

Large store retailers like Wal-Mart have been extremely successful in Mexico. In 2009, that organization had nearly 1,500 stores producing sales of 250 billion pesos (equivalent to about U.S. $20 billion) in Mexico (*source*: www.walmart.com/mexico_fact_sheet.pdf). However, Mexico's economic growth has been severely impacted by the recent global crisis, with real growth at −6.5 percent in 2009 (as compared to an average of +2.3 percent for the two preceding years); see www.cia .gov/library/publications/the-world-factbook.

Arnold is concerned about foreign exchange (FX) issues. His corporate treasurer, Bernie Paydoff, has no international experience; in fact Bernie hated to travel outside of the United States, although he had once been to Toronto. I. M. assured Arnold that the FX issue could be managed through forward contracts written by the bank to convert Mexican peso receipts into U.S. dollars. Furthermore, expenses such as payroll, local purchasing, and lease costs for the site would be paid in pesos and not U.S. dollars, so the extent of the FX conversion would be limited.

Arnold Sees an Information Gap

In discussing the Mexican option with Bernie, Arnold asked about the quality and usefulness of the information received from Second Chicago and other banks, and about the general nature of the bank relationships that Bernie saw in his work as corporate treasurer. Arnold believed that many things that had happened (see Parts I and II of this case) were due in part to the poor advice and inadequate information he had been given.

Bernie became somewhat defensive, claiming that he had done his job. While Arnold couldn't completely argue with this, he was concerned that Bernie was thinking of the treasurer's role as it was in 1980 and not the central focus of working capital management that it had become in many twenty-first-century companies. Based on comments from his banker, U. R. Clueless, and other Second Chicago officers, Arnold was beginning to consider the need for a major study of his information technology needs, particularly whether Internet-based bank technology would be the solution, as his bankers claimed, or if an enterprise resource planning (ERP) package should be considered.

Questions to Consider

Question 9. Is Arnold correct in his concerns? Will the cost of FX transaction exposure management offset the potential profits from this opportunity in Mexico?

Question 10. Are there other working capital issues Arnold should consider in deciding on a Mexican operation?

Question 11. Should Arnold seriously consider either the Second Chicago bank technology (called "Second Cash") or an ERP program, such as those offered by SAP and Oracle? What are the initial steps in deciding on an appropriate course of action?

CHAPTER 8

International Working Capital

After reading this material you will be able to:

- Consider the working capital opportunities in international business.
- Be aware of the financing of international transactions.
- Appreciate the basic concepts of foreign exchange.
- Evaluate country risk and other issues in international working capital.

U ntil about 25 years ago, some finance texts would not have included a section on international working capital. U.S. companies had been active in world trade beginning at about the end of World War I. However, companies such as IBM, General Motors, and Coca-Cola that found global opportunities often raised capital at home; owned and controlled their foreign operations; and often paid their employees, vendors, and government taxes in the strongest currency in the world, the U.S. dollar.

Starting at about the time of the 1973–1974 OPEC oil embargo, the U.S. Department of Commerce realized that American business had to substantially increase exports in order to pay for oil and other imports, and developed initiatives to improve participation in global trade. In the ensuing time, the U.S. dollar steadily declined in value (with brief periods of appreciation against other currencies); companies make and receive payments in local currencies; capital is raised wherever the cost is lowest; and U.S. companies actively seek foreign joint venture partners.

Capitalism Goes Global

American companies originally demanded ownership over foreign operations. The primary motives were to keep all of the profits and to absolutely control activities thousands of miles away on the theory that "the home office knows best." It took years of business mistakes and some hostile governments and/or local agitation for multinational corporations to learn their lesson.

Regardless of political orientation, nearly all international markets operate on capitalistic principles. This is an advantage for participants, permitting the following:

- *Global sourcing of capital for borrowers and investors:* This opportunity is particularly important in developing economies where the financial markets may not be as sophisticated as in the United States, Western Europe, or Japan.

- *Reduced risk for providers of capital:* The nearly unlimited investment alternatives in global markets allow lenders and investors to spread their risk exposures and achieve portfolio diversification of business assets.

- *Private enterprise:* The privatization movement that British Prime Minister Margaret Thatcher began in the 1970s has spread to nearly every country. Government-owned enterprises that were inefficient and stodgy are now owned by investors who seek profits through improved customer satisfaction and innovation.

- *Deregulation:* Beginning at about the same time, the financial markets moved toward deregulation. This development has increased competition, reduced fees and interest rate charges, encouraged the use of technology, and allowed the development of international policies to prevent financial crises.

Elements of International Working Capital

Practices vary significantly in the management of international working capital. The "point" person in many companies is the global treasury manager with responsibilities to manage banking relations, foreign exchange, and other cash-related activities. Other elements of working capital are often overlooked, and the level of management attention may decline to far below that of equivalent domestic activity. For example, collecting payments on outstanding invoices may require 40 days in the United States; in some countries the typical receivables period can be more than twice that time.

Global Working Capital Initiatives

An important global development has been the recent demand for transparency and ethical behavior. The 2008–2009 global credit crisis increased the expectation of responsible corporate behavior with the position of international finance (including working capital) elevated to be advisory to senior management.

The United States began this initiative with the Sarbanes-Oxley Act of 2002 (SOX), which was enacted as a reaction to a number of major corporate and accounting scandals. These losses cost investors billions of dollars when the share prices of affected companies collapsed, shaking public confidence in the securities markets. Two relevant sections of SOX deal with:

- *Corporate responsibility:* Title III mandates that senior executives take responsibility for the accuracy and completeness of corporate financial reports. It enumerates specific limits on the behaviors of corporate officers and describes specific forfeitures of benefits and civil penalties for noncompliance.

- *Enhanced financial disclosures:* Title IV requires enhanced reporting requirements for financial transactions, including off-balance-sheet transactions, pro forma figures, and stock transactions of corporate officers. It specifies internal controls for assuring the accuracy of financial reports and disclosures, and mandates both audits and reports on those controls.

Working capital practices vary by country; globalization is an intriguing concept but will require decades to accomplish. Many developed country business services firms have made significant profits by locating in developing economies near major corporations. Do not expect to find support for working capital initiatives from local vendors; for example, you are unlikely to find counterparties for JIT, factoring, or electronic payment systems in many countries.

Financing of International Transactions

With domestic transactions, financial managers attempt to optimize liquidity and efficiency. In contrast, global finance focuses on risk (to be discussed in Chapter 10), particularly the impact of foreign exchange and other exposures. *Foreign exchange* (FX) is the conversion of one currency to another currency. The most important form of financing—which will be discussed later in this section—is the letter of credit, which mitigates the risk of selling to customers in foreign markets we don't know.

Global Financial Risks

A company doing business internationally is typically exposed to any or all of the following types of risk.

- *Transaction exposure* is due to a movement in FX rates between the time a transaction is booked and the time it settles, potentially impacting the value of the deal. For example, if the euro weakens over the next month, the value of a euro receivable due in 30 days will be worth less in U.S. dollars when paid than the value today.

- *Translation exposure* is the balance sheet exposure that results when a company consolidates its financial statements and then reports the change in the net value of its foreign currency assets. The exposure results from fluctuations in FX, which change the rate at which net assets are valued.

- *Economic exposure* refers to the impact of fluctuating exchange rates on the value of future cash flows from long-term contracts. The longer the term of the contract, the greater the exposure.

Letter of Credit Concepts

As noted above, the principal method to mitigate credit risk in international transactions is the *letter of credit* (LC). The buyer requests an LC from an international bank that guarantees that the bank will pay the seller (or exporter) when the conditions of the LC are fulfilled. The bank requires that the buyer is known to the bank, or that an equivalent value of collateral is deposited to ensure that the bank will be fully compensated for the amount it finances. In essence, the bank substitutes its credit for that of the buyer.

Most LCs are irrevocable, where terms can be modified only if both the buyer and seller approve. Banks providing LCs are compensated by a fee (usually in the hundreds of dollars) paid by the buyer. However, the extensive document management involved in an LC often costs the bank as much as the fee received. This burden has been alleviated in recent years as banks have placed the LC forms on their secure web site, requiring the buyer to do most of the necessary paperwork.[1]

---

1. To view the LCs of international banks, see www.key.com/pdf/sampleloc.pdf or www.jpmorgan.com/cm/cs?pagename=JPM/DirectDoc&urlname=bd_loc_standby_app.pdf.

Letter of Credit Documentation

Following the issuance of the LC, the buyer's bank informs the seller's bank that the goods may be shipped. The seller must deliver a set of documents to its bank as required by the LC, which usually includes the following:

- An invoice.

- Any required governmental documents approving the transaction.

- A packing list.

- An inspection certificate.

- Proof of insurance.

- A *bill of lading*, which is a contract for shipment indicating that the goods are in transport to the buyer and proof of ownership.

When the seller's bank is satisfied that the documents meet the terms of the LC, the seller receives payment (see Exhibit 8.1). The buyer's bank approves of the contents of these documents, and pays the seller's bank. At that point, the buyer's bank expects reimbursement from the buyer.

Some transactions do occur on open credit where the buyer (or importer) is known to the seller or where credit reports are available. Where the buyer is not known, selling companies may demand a substantial portion or all of the payment in advance ("cash in advance").

Foreign Exchange Markets

So far we have been assuming that the buyer and seller in an international transaction are operating in a currency acceptable to both buyer and seller, be it a major world currency—the U.S. \$, the € (euro), the British £, or the Japanese ¥—or any of the other currencies used throughout the world. However, transactions may be in a currency that is not readily available to the buyer or

EXHIBIT 8.1

Letter of Credit Documentation Flow

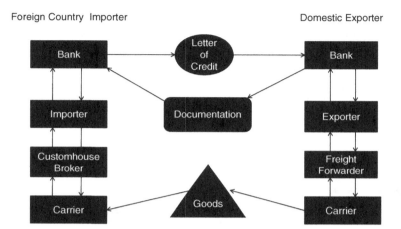

These steps in normal chronological order are as follows:

1. Exporter (seller) and importer (buyer) agree on conditions of sale.

2. Importer requests its bank to open a letter of credit.

3. Importer's bank prepares a letter of credit and sends it to the exporter's bank.

4. The importer's bank confirms the LC and transmits it to the exporter (its customer).

5. The exporter reviews the LC and arranges to deliver the goods to the importer through a freight forwarder.

6. The carrier prepares a bill of lading; other documents are prepared by the insurance company, the exporter (the invoice), and the appropriate government official (perhaps a certificate of origin). All documents are accumulated by the exporter.

7. The exporter presents the documents to its bank.

8. The exporter's bank reviews the documents, and if in order, credits the exporter's bank account.

9. The exporter's bank couriers or e-mails the documents to the importer's bank, which presents them to the importer and debits the importer's bank account

10. The importer presents the documents to the customhouse broker and receives the goods.

infrequently received by the seller, and either party may decide to convert those funds into its "home" currency. FX involves the largest and most liquid markets in the world, operating on a nearly 24/7 basis.

FX Mechanisms

FX allows the conversion of one currency to another through any of several mechanisms designed to meet the needs of a company engaged in international business.

- *Spot rates* are FX for delivery in two business days. ("Cash rates" are for same-day FX delivery.) The spot rate is the FX that is most often quoted in the financial newspapers; for example, the rates for early April 2010 are shown in Exhibit 8.2. Spot rates are used to

EXHIBIT 8.2

Selected FX Rates (for April 2, 2010)

	Foreign Currency in U.S. $	U.S. $ in Foreign Currency*
Australia (dollar)	0.919	1.088
Canada (dollar)	0.989	1.011
1 month forward	0.989	1.011
3 months forward	0.989	1.011
6 months forward	0.988	1.012
China (renminbi)	0.147	6.826
Europe (euro)	1.349	0.741
India (rupee)	0.022	44.76
Japan (yen)	0.011	94.56
1 month forward	0.011	94.54
3 months forward	0.011	94.51
6 months forward	0.011	94.43
Mexico (peso)	0.081	12.30
Russia (ruble)	0.034	29.26
Switzerland (franc)	0.942	1.062
UK (pound)	1.521	0.658
1 month forward	1.520	0.658
3 months forward	1.520	0.658
6 months forward	1.519	0.658

Note: These are currency trades in amounts of $1 million or more as quoted by various sources. For sources of FX quotes, see Exhibit 3.5.
*Where the convention is to state the U.S. $ in the quantity of the foreign currency, this is indicated in an italicized FX quote.

settle business transactions; retail transactions are in much smaller quantities and are not as favorable as spot rates.

- *Forward rates* are hedging instruments[2] used for the delivery of the FX on a specified later date, and are used by businesses to "lock in" a rate when it is likely that an international transaction will settle in the future (i.e., in 30 or 60 days). Forwards are available from international banks and the largest FX dealers, and are written for specific amounts and dates negotiated between the company and the bank. A company—the buyer—would consider using a forward contract when there is concern that the home currency may lose value in the coming period (FX risk) and that waiting to buy spot FX may cost more at the time that payment must be made.

  Here's an example: Your company owes 100,000 £ in three months, and you are concerned that your home currency, the U.S. $, will decrease in value (as it did through much of 2007–2008). As of early April 2010, a forward contract can be executed at $1.5197 locking in that rate. In addition, the FX dealer will charge a small commission. (*Note*: The spot rate for the £ on that date was $1.5206.)

- *Futures contracts* are available through American commodities exchanges. Futures are similar to forwards in that the FX is for delivery of FX at a later date. However, these contracts are based on standard-sized contracts rather than tailored to a company's specific requirement and are written for delivery on specified dates. For example, the standard size contract for £ is 62,500 £, which were trading at $1.520 for three-month delivery. The contract sizes for other major currencies are CD $100,000 (Canada), €125,000, ¥12.5 million, and 500,000 Mexican pesos. These contracts are listed on the Chicago Mercantile Exchange and are traded on a company's behalf by a commodities broker.

---

2. Hedging was defined in Chapter 6.

The forward or future FX rate differs slightly from the spot rate due to market expectations regarding the specific currency. Forwards (or futures) may be greater or less than the spot rate; for example, £ forwards sell at a slight discount from the spot rate, possibly in anticipation of an interest rate cut by the Bank of England. For a discussion of recent

IN THE REAL WORLD

Continuous Link Settlement versus Spot FX

Foreign exchange markets have traditionally settled on a "spot" basis, that is, two business days ahead. A new system called Continuous Link Settlement (CLS) is a process by which a number of large banks manage settlement of foreign exchange among themselves (and their customers and other third parties). Since it began operations, CLS has become the market standard for foreign exchange settlement between major banks.

The motivation behind CLS was to eliminate the risk associated with cross-currency transactions, specifically referred to as Herstatt risk, named after the German bank that almost caused the collapse of the banking system in 1974. Herstatt's Luxembourg Branch declared bankruptcy and failed to settle its foreign exchange contracts.

The currencies that settle through CLS include:

Australian Dollar	New Zealand Dollar
Canadian Dollar	Singapore Dollar
Danish Krone	South African Rand
Euro	South Korean Won
Hong Kong Dollar	Swedish Krona
Israeli New Shekel	Swiss Franc
Japanese Yen	Pound Sterling
Mexican Peso	United States Dollar

developments in FX, see *In the Real World: Continuous Link Settlement versus Spot FX.*

Factors Influencing FX Rates

With a few exceptions (such as certain currencies from Middle Eastern countries), the FX markets float without intervention by central banks or other government agencies. This situation has existed since the early 1970s when the U.S. dollar was taken off of the gold standard that had been established in 1944 at the Bretton Woods (NH) conference. At that time, the U.S. $ was convertible at 1/35 ounce of gold on demand; however, the diminishing reserves of American gold forced the Nixon Administration to stop redeeming $ for gold on demand from foreign holders of $.

There are various influences on FX rates, and at any given time, one or another drives rates higher or lower against other rates. The most important influences are the following:

- *Inflation:* Differences in purchasing power due to inflationary pressures are an important influence on FX.

- *Interest rates:* High interest rates tend to make a currency attractive as investors seek higher returns; lower rates, as the United States experienced in early 2008, caused the U.S. $ to decline against other major currencies.

- *Balance of payments:* The calculation of trade and other government transfers constitutes a country's balance of payments; chronic deficits usually cause a currency to decline relative to other FX.

- *Government spending and taxation:* The FX markets react positively to a country's efforts to maintain stability between taxing and spending.

These factors operate over a long cycle and are not reliable for short-term FX forecasts that most international transactions require. However, it is instructive to note the experience of the U.S. $ in the period before the credit crisis that began in 2008. From early 2005 to 2008, the U.S. $ fell against the £ from $1.88 to $1.99 or 6.3 percent; against the € from $1.29 to $1.58 or 22.8 percent; and against the ¥ from 104.02 to 99.21 or 4.6 percent. Recent changes in the £ and the € reflect the very weak economic conditions in those areas. Even more alarming, the U.S. $ had declined about 40 percent against the major currencies since the beginning of the twenty-first century (as of the beginning of the current credit crisis).[3] The deteriorating position of the U.S. economy during that time was directly reflected in the value of its currency.

Multicurrency Accounts

FX can be managed using a single international bank account with the capability to receive deposits and withdrawals of several major currencies; this facility is often called a *multicurrency account*. These centralized currency accounts are easy to set up and maintain; there is one set of account-opening documentation, low maintenance fees, and a single point of contact for customer service. The disadvantage is that a currency handled in a country other than that of its domicile (e.g., £ in France) may be subject to availability delays upon deposit and up to two days' delay on transfer. Cross-border currency transfers are usually done on a spot basis.

Electronic Payments

Many developed economies have made significant progress toward electronic payment instruments.[4] The United Kingdom recently announced that it had set a target date of October 2018 to stop the central clearing of checks, which have declined in use by about two-thirds from the peak in 1990. The abolition of checking in Britain would produce annual

---

3. Estimate by Alan Abelson, "The True Contrarians," *Barron's Newspaper*, March 31, 2008, pp. 6–8. The period 2008–2010 has been an anomaly in the long economic cycle, particularly as the U.S. $ is perceived as a "safe haven" in times of credit and banking crises.

4. For a discussion of international electronic payment mechanisms, see Michele Allman-Ward and James Sagner, *Essentials of Managing Corporate Cash*, Chapter 7 (Hoboken, NJ: John Wiley & Sons, Inc., 2003).

savings of nearly £1 billion and prevent the destruction of nearly 50,000 trees.[5] The lead of the U.K. on this issue and the rise of the "green movement" could spread to other economies, particularly other EU countries.

In a related initiative, the Single Euro Payments Area (SEPA) will enable making cashless euro payments to any party located in the euro area using a single bank account and set of payment instruments. All retail payments will become "domestic" as there will no longer be any differentiation between national and cross-border payments within the euro area. The implementation of SEPA is ongoing, with milestone events currently in progress.[6]

Analysis of Country Risk

Country (or sovereign) risk is the possibility that a foreign government will interfere with normal business transactions between counterparties due to an economic or political crisis. Examples of such actions include the debt moratoria declared by the Brazilian and Mexican governments in the early 1980s, the financial problems of various Asian countries in the late 1990s, and the 2010 crisis in Greece. Country stability can be monitored through evaluation models published by *The Economist, Euromoney*, Business Monitor International, and other sources.

Country risk assessment (CRA) quantifies the possibility that transactions with international counterparties may be interrupted by the interference of the foreign government or due to local conditions through the analysis of political and economic risks. Such disruptions may take the form of prohibitions or limitations on currency flows due to economic problems or political reasons. There were several examples of such outcomes in the 1980s and 1990s in parts of South America,

---

5. See "The Demise of the Cheque," House of Commons, document dated Feb. 10, 2010, at www .parliament.uk/commons/lib/research/briefings/SNBT-05318.pdf.
6. For further information, see www.ecb.int/paym/sepa/html/index.en.html.

Mexico, Russia, and several Far Eastern countries. Countries with recent problems include Spain, Portugal, and Iceland.

Country Risk Experience

As an illustration of a specific situation, several Asian nations, following Japan's lead, pursued economic practices contrary to those of free market nations. This included overinvesting in factories making products that could not be sold at a profit; oversaving, which dampened the extremely important economic stimulus of consumer spending; overregulating, which distorted the discipline provided by global competition; and (at least in Japan) the cultural tradition of *giri ninjo*, or the retention of inefficient business practices because of feelings of commitment and empathy toward workers and the community.

In contrast, Western economies have generally encouraged investment but have never assumed that production surpluses could be managed through exporting and planned trade surpluses; have undersaved according to many economists, certainly as reflected in the trillions of dollars of outstanding U.S. debt; and have moved decisively toward deregulation. This is a significant consideration because of the promotion of international business through the World Trade Organization (WTO). The emergence of China has energized the Western economies to seek global opportunities with seemingly huge potential.

Country risk exists when you do business in any sovereign nation, in that the rules and laws you depend on could change or be unenforceable in a dispute. China and other countries may appear attractive, but working capital managers must be knowledgeable about the country risk. Political, economic, or social instability could disrupt business operations in developing countries, particularly in times of recession or mediocre economic growth.

Other Significant Issues in International Working Capital

We noted that the traditional model in organizing for international finance was to direct activities on a centralized basis from the home office. Inefficiencies and delays in accessing markets and in responding to changing conditions have refocused finance to various forms of regional management.

Structures to Manage FX

Two popular FX management structures are tax-advantaged centers and reinvoicing centers.

- *Tax advantaged centers:* Several countries offer low corporate taxes and other benefits to attract multinationals, anticipating that they will establish offices for the management of their various business functions including finance. In return, the local economy receives economic activity and employment. Among these centers are the International Financial Services Company (IFSC) in Ireland, the Belgian Coordination Center (BCC), Swiss and Luxembourg Holding Companies, and Singapore's Operational Headquarters (OHQ).

  The search for continued efficiencies has led to India, the Philippines, and the Czech Republic all becoming increasingly popular locations for these centers. *Tips and Techniques: EU Tax-Advantaged Centers* reviews the status of these centers in the European Union countries as of mid-2010.

- *Reinvoicing centers:* These are centralized financial subsidiaries used by multinational companies to reduce transaction exposure. All home country exports are billed in the home country currency and reinvoiced to each operating affiliate in that affiliate's local currency. Business units do not deal directly with each other, but place their orders through the center. Although title passes to the

EU Tax-Advantaged Centers

Tax-advantaged centers may eventually be eliminated in the EU, as efforts toward tax harmonization proceed. (*Harmonization* is the enactment of laws in different jurisdictions, such as neighboring countries, that are consistent with one another.) The EU has discussed such policy as tax rates and practices vary significantly across member countries. Although no action is likely to occur until the world economy is clearly in recovery, these centers face pressure to be eliminated in favor of standardization and the harmonization of tax regimes. Companies seeking tax benefits may be forced to consider locations outside of the EU.

center,[7] the goods are shipped directly to the purchasing subsidiary. The center gives the multinational enhanced control over international flows while providing both quantitative and qualitative benefits. These include management of FX exposure and improved global working capital management.

Cross-Border Clearing and Settlement

Delays are nearly always involved in cross-border transactions, primarily because currencies must eventually settle in their country of origin. There are various examples where a foreign currency (usually the U.S. dollar) is widely used in a local economy, and arrangements have been made to clear locally drawn and payable items offshore.

The U.K. Currency Clearing system clears checks drawn and payable in the City of London in the currencies of the U.S., Canada, Australia, Japan, and Switzerland. Singapore, Hong Kong, the Philippines, and Canada all clear electronic payments and checks in U.S. dollars.

---

7. The concept of *title* refers to the ownership of an asset; in this case, the goods being sold.

Ultimately the currencies will settle across correspondent accounts in their country of domicile; for example, British pounds will settle in the U.K.

Trade transactions are covered by a well-established, internationally recognized body of rules and regulations issued by the International Chamber of Commerce (ICC). Although the United Nations and the European Community (EC) are currently attempting to establish limited international guidelines, cross-border movements of cash at present are not subject to any internationally accepted codes of performance.

Cultural and Corporate Practices Affecting Working Capital

Western businesspeople generally do not have enough exposure to international cultures and corporate practices to easily transfer their business activities to foreign countries, particularly where English is not the primary language. A major source of past mistakes has been the arrogance of U.S executives who were certain that their successes would be repeated in European, Asian, or other societies. Here are some other complexities that need to be considered:[8]

Cultural Differences

Among the various cultural differences between countries are:

- Different holidays, weekends, and religious practices can significantly limit common business days and delay cross-border transfers.

- Payment preferences may vary; many countries prefer to use electronic payment methods and paper transactions are unusual.

- Payment terms differ. For example, Scandinavian countries usually have credit terms of 15 to 30 days; other countries, such as Italy and Spain, stretch terms out 90 to 120 days.

---

8. This listing of international complexities is based on Allman-Ward and Sagner, op. cit., footnote 4.

- "Getting right down to business" is not always appreciated and may even be regarded as offensive; business discussions may need to be prefaced with an obligatory "small talk" or entertainment session.

Banking Practices

Banking practices differ between countries in several ways:

- Banking systems of the world vary in structure and have limited cross-border connectivity. Countries have different rules as to who may open accounts and can be authorized signers.

- Bank compensation often varies from U.S. practice; in particular, value dating[9] may be used. Other practices include turnover fees, with some countries charging fees based on a percentage of the value of the activity (debit or credit) in the account; ad valorem charges, based on a percentage of the value of the transaction; and fixed annual charges for access to a high value payment system.

- *Pooling* is offered by many banks; in this arrangement, debit and credit balances of a company's separate accounts are offset daily to calculate a net balance with the bank paying or charging interest on the net debit or credit.

- *Netting* is a process that allows entities to offset their total receivables against their total payables, with each entity either receiving or paying the net amount to the netting center in their local currency.

Communications Infrastructure

The differences in communications infrastructure include:

- Certain developing countries are not able to support the level of technology used in the United States and other developed countries.

---

9. *Value dating* is a bank practice of taking days of value as a form of compensation. Forward value dating is when the receiving bank provides available funds on an incoming credit one or two business days forward. With back value dating, the originating bank will back value the debit to the account by one or two business days.

- Data lines may not be available or robust enough for long-distance transmissions.

- A continuous flow of electricity cannot be assumed in certain locations.

Legal and Tax Issues

The differences in legal and tax issues include:

- Some countries have exchange controls that prohibit the free flow of funds outside the country, or require laborious paperwork to document a transfer of funds.

- Taxes will likely be due on revenues generated in the local country; the extent to which they are deductible against income on the consolidated financials will depend on whether there is a double taxation treaty.[10]

Time Zones and Language Barriers

Among the time zone and language barriers are:

- Time zones can have a considerable impact on how working capital is managed. Most companies prefer to organize on a regional basis, ensuring local expertise and a reasonable time span in which to operate.

- Instructions may not be correctly interpreted, problem resolution can be difficult and account-opening forms can be difficult to understand.

- Although much of the international business world speaks some English, cultural biases and colloquial nuances may result in a different interpretation of a conversation, even between English-speaking people.

---

10. A *double taxation treaty* stipulates the rates at which taxes will be levied between two countries and whether taxes paid in one can be offset against taxes due in the other.

Summary

Global working capital management emphasizes risk rather than efficiency (as is the focus in domestic finance), particularly the impact of foreign exchange. The major risks that must be managed are transaction, translation, and economic exposures, and various methods are discussed that allow financial managers to reduce these concerns. International finance is conducted in a cultural and corporate environment that is often at variance from domestic practice, and several of these issues were reviewed.

This chapter also discussed letters of credit and other mechanisms available to reduce the risk of selling to international customers whose creditworthiness is uncertain. Country risk assessment was reviewed, which allows managers to understand concerns in doing business in specific countries.

CHAPTER 9

Information and Working Capital*

After reading this chapter, you will be able to:

- Understand how working capital information products are used to communicate between information providers and its business clients.

- Review features, benefits, and disadvantages of Internet-based bank technology.

- Analyze enterprise resource planning (ERP) as a more comprehensive approach to developing working capital information.

- Develop a strategy for the selection of a working capital information system.

As we have reported throughout this book, the management of working capital is complex—involving many different tasks, organizational functions, and sources of information. Fortunately, developments in computer technologies and communications make these activities relatively user-friendly and efficient, with banks and vendors offering integrated platforms requiring secure access to business

*This chapter was coauthored with Arthur McAdams; for further information, see the Acknowledgments.

175

users. We will first review the standard bank technology, discuss ERP systems, and then note customary phases of the selection process.

Information Technology

Technology is not magic! Systems that support working capital functionality are like all sources of information: Successful applications require good management. For any technology to succeed, it must work in harmony with the people and processes in its organizational function. While many information systems may use a fair amount of their output (volume) capacity, most only use a fraction of their features (functionality).

Far too often, technology can be employed as a remedy for intellectual laziness, in which an organization hands its unresolved problems over to a software vendor with the hope of a miraculous and inexpensive remedy. Technology can also create its own self-serving universe within certain circles and take on a life—complete with insider language and culture—of its own. This can distract attention away from the purpose of the application to the intricacies of the tool.

Special Status of IT

Until the recent credit crisis, a significant issue in managing a business has been the special status of the information technology function, in that when new hardware or software is requested, it is usually approved. Few companies subjected these acquisitions to rigorous evaluation, and information products were approved based on little more than faith. This situation is changing due to the need to carefully manage capital and the trend toward the outsourcing of technological applications.

Working capital issues to consider in any information technology decision include:

- Does the project meet the company's requirements? Large sums have been spent on systems that were never properly scoped and designed, and inevitably more money and time became necessary for even partial implementation. Supply chain management (SCM) systems (discussed in Chapter 6) have been problematic, as are applications that purport to analyze risk management (to be discussed in Chapter 10).

- Does the project have internal support (often referred to as a "champion") or is a vendor the major proponent? Technology vendors are talented at developing interest in a project that no one ever considered before, particularly as their compensation is often based on sales commissions. The internal supporter should be willing to stake his or her budget, credibility, time, and even career on a technology success.

- External solutions can appear to be reasonably inexpensive; after all, the vendor may have priced the technology at $5,000 to $10,000 a month. However, there are many other costs to consider, including parallel testing, implementation, training, staffing, special facilities requirements, documentation, security, additional computing and communications equipment, establishing second sites in the event of a disaster, and other expenditures. The investment only begins with the acquisition of the system. Some costs will directly impact working capital, while others will be depreciated over the expected life of the technology.

- Has our company considered outsourcing the project to an application service provider (ASP)? An *ASP* is a business that sells access to software applications through central servers over a communications network. ASP providers include IBM, Oracle/BEA Systems, and hundreds of other companies, some of which focus on the computing requirements of specific industries. Major advantages include the following:

  - The ASP's core competency is to support the technology requirements of its clients for a reasonable monthly fee.

- Costs are significantly lower than developing, owning, supporting, creating a backup site, and upgrading a complete system.

Disadvantages of ASPs are significant:

- Specific client requirements cannot be supported except at significant cost.

- Clients may rely on the ASP to provide a critical business function, which limits their control of that function.

- The ASP could decide to limit or terminate the service.

- There could be a change in management support, ownership, or even failure of the ASP.

Bank Information Technology

Bank information products allow companies to electronically access a full range of financial services and to execute many types of transactions, activities previously available only by personal contact, or through separate and costly computer systems. The menu of possible actions is fairly extensive; listed in the following section are modules providing standard and advanced services.

Basic Transactional Functionality

At the most basic level, bank systems are used to optimize and expedite the transactions required to conduct business. In other words, these systems promote information flow, which also often has the side benefit of convenience, without losing accuracy or compromising security, privacy, or regulatory compliance. Since most commercial software provides the basic transactional functionality, any automated differentiation must be realized by setting system parameters. This is an important requirement in your search if you plan on offering a unique product or service supported by the technology.

Many bank systems are accessible internally and externally using Internet technology. The immediate and seamless delivery of information has improved efficiency and offered banks, and their customers, great gains in service. This exponential growth in functionality makes the basic management of working capital fairly routine. However, the technology used by the bank is important to the customer because access will be required through firewalls, security restrictions, and other safeguards.

Modules for Standard Services

The following modules provide the standard reporting services required by many companies. The term *reporting* refers to information summaries and details of bank account activity.

- *Balance and activity.* Yesterday's and today's ledger and available balances are listed in these reports, including details of debits and credits, float by day (zero, one, and two business days), and other transactions. Companies use these data to begin the periodic (often daily) process of developing a cash budget. Banks run their demand deposit account (DDA) systems (from which much of this information is derived) at night, with previous-day activity available the next morning. As same-day reporting requires feeds from separate systems and is more costly to provide, there is usually a premium charge for this service. DDAs and cash budgets were discussed in Chapter 3.

- *Polling and parsing.* Account data can be retrieved by *polling* banks electronically and then downloading or *parsing* information into reports based on a script developed at the time of installation. Important features include the following:

  - Automatic dialing of banks.
  - Electronic responses through scripts.
  - Selection of appropriate data.

- Formatting into reports.

- Exception reports of banks for whom information was unavailable.

- *Wire transfer.* As discussed in Chapter 2, wire transfers are same-day, final transfers used primarily for large dollar transactions. Appropriate practice for control and security strongly encourages that these transactions be initiated, approved, and released through a bank's software (rather than by telephone or fax), using keys and passwords unique to the sender and receiver. In fact, the few recent cases of fraudulent wire transactions involved manual wires, and some banks charge as much as $100 per manual wire to discourage such activity.

- *Automated Clearing House (ACH).* Many banks now offer terminal-based ACH, allowing debit and credit transfers to be initiated by finance rather than through the mainframe computer system. This permits flexibility in sending and receiving payments for a low fee, and allows the initiation of ACHs or intrabank transfers to cover the daily clearing amount in controlled disbursement accounts.

- *Controlled disbursement.* Information modules offer various electronic reporting options, including stop payments (for checks issued in error), the transmission of checks issued files (for positive pay review and monthly reconciliation), the review of positive pay mismatches, and account reconciliation data.

- *Multibank reporting.* Bank systems can generally consolidate balance and transaction activity from a company's banking network, simplifying the task and reducing the cost of retrieving these data from each bank.

- *Bank relationship management.* A useful module includes information on bank relationships and contacts including:

  - Name, address, telephone, and fax numbers.

  - Names of senior managers, calling officers, and customer service staff.

- History of the relationship and calling efforts.

- Listing of services used, persistent problems, and unique capabilities.

- Credit facilities available and used, as well as fees, restrictions, and other covenants.

Modules for Advanced Services

Larger banks offer additional modules designed to meet the needs of companies doing business globally.

- *Foreign exchange (FX).* Banks offer modules to expedite the process of purchasing or selling FX, primarily in the major currencies used in international transactions. Other FX may be available based on the market presence of each bank and the requirements of its corporate customers. In addition to automating FX transactions, these modules offer lower transaction charges and better rates than by manually contacting financial institutions.

- *Letters of credit (LCs).* Export and import financing often requires bank LCs to assure payment once all documentation and other requirements have been completed (see Chapter 8). LC modules enable automated processing of the LC and supporting documentation.

- *International money transfer.* Funds movement between global banks involves linking various different international money transfer systems, usually using SWIFT formats.[1] In addition, extensive cross-border payment capabilities help companies manage payments globally through a single message to your bank.

- *Investment management.* Portfolios of investments can be managed by listing short- and long-term holdings, including trades,

---

1. SWIFT messages allow a "host" electronic banking platform to act as the conduit to transmit wire transfer messages to other banks. SWIFT is an acronym for Society for Worldwide Interbank Financial Telecommunications. For further information, see www.swift.com.

marked-to-market pricing, and the tracking of dividends, interest, and other income. Larger financial institutions offer a full array of products, including:

- Automated sweep services.

- Fixed income securities.

- Money market funds.

- Tax advantaged investments.

- Managed account solutions.

- *Debt management.* Debt modules report credit line activity, commercial paper outstanding, fixed and floating rate instruments, and intercompany loans. Global capabilities may include pooling, a technique used by in-house banks (often located in treasury centers) to offset the deficits in the accounts of certain subsidiaries with excess cash in the accounts of other subsidiaries, and netting, involving the reduction in the number of intracompany payments through the consolidation and aggregation of individual transactions. These techniques were discussed in Chapter 8.

Internet Bank Technology

The widespread use of the Internet has evolved to the current situation where banks have backed away from product technology support. This development has occurred due to the cost of the expertise and equipment, and to the difficulty of keeping products current with the rapidly evolving customer demands. A number of banks use systems provided by P & H Solutions (formerly Politzer and Haney)[2], FISERV,[3] and other ASP vendors. See Exhibit 9.1 for selected functionalities provided to banks by these ASPs.

---

2. For case studies of bank and corporate P & H applications, see the web site of their parent company, ACI Worldwide, at www.aciworldwide.com/igsbase/igstemplate.cfm/SRC=SP/SRCN=sharedcontent_casestudies_overview/GnavID=29/SnavID=79.

3. For additional information, see www.fiserv.com.

EXHIBIT 9.1

Bank Internet Technology Features

Business intelligence

Compliance

Cross-selling capability and client support

Document management and imaging

End-to-end bank platforms

Image technology

Integrated risk management

Multichannel customer sales and service

New account setup

Online banking

Relational databases

Secure online banking channels and transactions

Straight-through processing

Teller, business intelligence, mobile, and Internet banking

Entry to bank Internet-based systems is through a standard Web browser, allowing the menu of financial services to be accessible at any time and in all locations. As a result, the finance manager is no longer tied to a specific PC loaded with the bank's proprietary software. This allows mobile computing in situations when staff are traveling, when other personnel must review a transaction, or if a disaster were to prevent entry to the usual office location. For a situation where this occurs, see *In the Real World: Involve the Responsible Organizational Function in Banking Decisions.*

Benefits of Internet Bank Technology

There are various advantages to the use of Internet-based technology services:

- *Cost.* A full range of modules is available to users at a nominal cost. Automating bank transactions greatly reduces costs for personnel, technology, and customer service, and presents a suite of technology services previously unavailable to many small- and medium-sized companies.

IN THE REAL WORLD

Involve the Responsible Organizational Function in Banking Decisions

Check mismatches (where the issued and clearing check numbers and/or amounts due not match) occur due to errors by company or bank personnel, or because the recipient or a thief has altered the check. Banks provide a service called positive pay to find these situations and report them to the issuing company, with a time limit on whether or not to honor the check; see Chapter 2. The issuing function (e.g., accounts payable) can review positive pay files directly to determine if check mismatches should be honored or rejected.

Before the Internet-based platform became standard practice, this process was handled by finance staff, who were often uninformed as to the purpose or validity of a particular disbursement. The result was a series of telephone calls, e-mails, or faxes, and any delay meant that the period for review (usually only about four hours) might pass. In that situation, the bank decision reverts to the preset "accept" or "reject" rule made by the company at the time the account was established, and that default is almost always "accept."

Other functions in a company similarly require data from banks that can be viewed using the Internet. For example, sales managers want to ship but experience slow-paying customers that present a risk to the collection of receivables. With access to lockbox receipts, they can quickly determine whether payments have been received and if it is appropriate to ship against pending orders.

- *Secure single platform access.* Access through a single platform allows the corporate user to move easily from one product to another. Security is provided through 128-bit transport layer security (TLL) protocols,[4] multiple levels of user IDs, monitoring by the bank, and various other controls.

- *Ease of implementation and upgrading.* New modules can be installed with minimal setup, delivery effort, and cost. User-friendly menus enable users to quickly learn and adopt new technology, and banks provide online tutorials to allow on-demand training and unlimited repetitions. There is no requirement for physical installation of software, as the information modules reside on the bank's server.

- *Disaster recovery.* Banks have multiple backup sites for their computer services, and these locations are widely dispersed to avoid the risk of a catastrophe affecting more than one data center. These facilities are frequently stress tested for reactions to emergency situations.

- *File exporting.* Working capital management is simplified through file exporting in various formats to support accounting, receivables, payables, and inventory management. However, the working capital file interfaces are not integrated in a common platform as are ERP systems.

- *Reports.* Companies can receive summary and detailed reports on every service, each user, by product, and by bank account. Control is enhanced through this reporting and the archiving of activity; see Chapter 8 for a comment on the control requirements of the Sarbanes-Oxley Act of 2002.

Disadvantages of Internet Bank Technology

Disadvantages include the following:

- *Noncore competency.* Many banks would prefer not to allocate the required capital or expertise to the design and maintenance of an Internet-based product. For this reason, ASPs have become the primary providers of bank technology. As the result, the bank does not "own" the product, the ASP does.

---

4. TLS and its predecessor secure-sockets-layer SSL are cryptographic procedures that provide security for communications over the Internet and other networks.

- *Service coverage.* The scope of functions offered by even the largest banks is limited to standard financial products.[5] As a result, information is not provided on the other working capital functions as listed in Exhibit 9.2.

EXHIBIT 9.2

Working Capital Lines of Business Features (for typical ERP systems)

Finance

- Accelerate closing of financial statements
- Optimize working capital
- Integrate and support functions for treasury and cash management

Asset management

- Improve visibility of company assets
- Enhance access to management of intellectual property
- Increase asset safety and compliance

Human resources

- Improve management of employees
- Control HR management costs

Environment, health, and safety

- Increase the ability to identify and mitigate environmental, health, and safety risks
- Streamline environmental, health, and safety processes
- Manage and report compliance for corporate safety policies

Manufacturing

- Synchronize global manufacturing fulfillment
- Increase efficiency in logistics and fulfillment processes

---

5. Regulation Y (12 *Code of Federal Regulations* 225.21) issued by the Federal Reserve prohibits banks from engaging in businesses that are beyond the scope of traditional banking activities. For this reason, it is unlikely (at least for the foreseeable future) that banks will offer information services that go beyond the standard concept of "cash."

- Manage configured products and service parts better
- Control the global network of suppliers

Marketing

- Optimize sales and marketing efforts
- Leverage insight to align marketing and sales activities
- Retain profitable customers

Procurement

- Streamline and centralize procure-to-payables processes
- Enforce comprehensive contract compliance
- Improve visibility into supplier performance
- Increase visibility of purchasing activities

Product development

- Accelerate delivery of innovative products to market
- Collaborate with partners in the delivery of safe products

Sales

- Implement sales strategies that promote growth
- Increase the efficiency of sales teams
- Accelerate sales cycles

Service

- Deliver superior customer service
- Quickly resolve customer problems
- Optimize the use of resources available for service
- Increase cross-selling and up-selling to existing customers

Supply chain management

- Respond to global supply and demand dynamics
- Synchronize supply and demand
- Leverage technologies to uniquely identify inventory
- Deal effectively with supply chain incidents like recalls

(*continued*)

▮ **EXHIBIT 9.2**
(continued)

Information technology

- Use information technology to increase enterprise competitiveness
- Lower total cost of ownership of technology
- Increase user satisfaction with installed software

Source: Derived from descriptions of SAP ERP systems at www.sap.com; Oracle ERP systems at www.oracle.com; and Sungard ERP systems (specifically for the public sector and educational institutions) at www.sungard.com.

Enterprise Resource Planning: An Alternative Approach

We introduced the topic of enterprise resource planning (ERP) in Chapter 7, defining the concept as an integrated approach to managing a company's resources. The coverage of an ERP installation is much broader than bank Internet technology, involving many of the working capital accounts discussed throughout this book. Furthermore, the extension of these applications into so many business activities goes far beyond traditional accounting system data, which focus on ledger entries in response to fairly rigid regulatory requirements, providing assistance to management in its decision-making activities.

Why ERP?

ERP responded to manager demands for information that would provide in-depth information on many working capital issues and help answer "what if"-type questions. Why are sales declining in a particular market? Why is this customer less profitable than that customer? What has been the sales outcome when prices rose or advertising expenditures fell? In order to accomplish this goal without creating individual systems for each company, ERP was organized around standard modules, requiring that existing business processes be mapped using a thorough business process analysis before selecting an ERP vendor and beginning implementation.

This analysis should document current operations, enabling the selection of an ERP vendor whose standard modules are most closely aligned with the established organization. Furthermore, ERP systems can extend beyond a single organization to support comprehensive business activities that cross a company's organizational, departmental, and geographic boundaries, including customers, suppliers, and partners.

Advantages of ERP

There are various advantages to the use of ERP:

- *Common interface.* A typical problem that companies face is the lack of a common interface between the various systems it uses. For example, accounting software does not interact with bank technology, while supply chain management involves an entirely different platform and data entry protocols. As we noted, files can only be interfaced through exporting protocols. ERP can end these "silos" and allow functional components of a business to communicate rather than be separate and focused on their own objectives.

- *Best practices.* Vendors use generally accepted "best practices" to design the modules that support ERP. These procedures assist inefficient companies in adapting effective approaches to specific business activities through the necessary redesign and reengineering that allow ERP to function.

- *Control of sensitive data.* ERP systems reduce the risk of the loss of sensitive data by combining multiple access permissions and security models into a single structure. Security features protect against outsider crime such as industrial espionage, and insider crime such as embezzlement.

- *Newer "light" versions of ERP.* Systems vendors have addressed some of the cost and implementation problems of ERP through the development of "ERP-light" technology. For a review of these

offerings, see www.whitepapers.org/land/erp-comparison-guide/
?tfso=5694.

Disadvantages of ERP

ERP systems are complex and usually impose significant changes on staff work practices. Implementing the process is typically too complicated for internal personnel, forcing companies to hire outside assistance to implement these systems. As a result of these complexities, there are three issues to consider particularly when compared to competitive bank technology as supported by internal systems.

1. *Modules require standardization.* ERP systems inherently require modular components based on standard business processes. Companies desiring to implement ERP must reconfigure existing activities to meet the system's requirements, and it is precisely the unique approach of a business that may have led to marketplace success. While there is nothing wrong with reengineering an established set of procedures,[6] the effort should provide clear added value.

2. *Time, cost, and other implementation issues.* The length of time to implement ERP can be greater than one year and involve both internal staff and consultants. The cost of an ERP can be $1 million or more considering software and consultant fees.[7] Any estimate of time and cost depends on the size of the business, the number of modules, the extent of customization, the scope of the business change, and the willingness of the company to take ownership for the project.

3. *Training.* Other than implementation, a considerable problem with ERP results from an inadequate effort in ongoing training. With bank systems, the training is focused on the user (and not on the

---

6. Indeed, the author's first book was titled *Cashflow Reengineering: How to Optimize the Cashflow Timeline and Improve Financial Efficiency* (New York: AMACOM, 1997).

7. "The Total Cost of ERP Ownership," Aberdeen Group, October 17, 2006, reported at www.oracle.com/corporate/analyst/reports/corporate/cp/es101306.pdf.

information technology function) through Internet downloads and tutorials. This avoids reengineering entire business processes, purchasing new generations of hardware and software, and other potential delays.

Choosing Working Capital Information Systems

The implementation of a working capital system should be constructed as a multiphase effort, with each phase logically following from the conclusions reached in the previous step. It is appropriate to remind readers that many information projects fail, and the culprit is poor management, not flawed technology.

The Standish Group, which has performed extensive research on project management for the last several decades, estimates that about two-thirds of these efforts fail because they do not meet at least one of the following three criteria: estimated completion date, anticipated cost, or promised features. In fact, most projects miss more than one of the criteria and all too often dates and costs are "met" by significantly

IN THE REAL WORLD

Information System Problems?
It's Easier to Unplug than Sue

In considering a working capital information system, remember that bank products are "plug and play"—that is, you have little implementation other than to comply with relatively simple bank protocols. Furthermore, these modules reside on bank computers (or on a third-party provider who actually sells and supports the system). If you are unhappy or dissatisfied with the product, you "unplug" and inform the bank to stop invoicing you.

ERP systems are major capital investments that cannot easily be abandoned. According to *CIO* magazine, the recent history of this software " . . . is packed with tales of vendor mud-slinging, outrageous hype, and epic failures."[a] A listing of dissatisfied companies includes Hershey Foods, Nike, Hewlett-Packard, and Select Comfort (bedding products). These situations resulted in losses in the hundreds of millions of dollars, unhappy customers, lawsuits, and other unfortunate outcomes.

[a] See Thomas Wailgum, "10 Famous ERP Disasters, Dustups and Disappointments," *CIO* magazine, March 24, 2009, at www.cio.com/article/486284/ 10_Famous_ERP_Disasters_Dustups_and_Disappointments.

overestimating the initial projection.[8] For further discussion, see *In the Real World: Information System Problems? It's Easier to Unplug than Sue.*

Phase 1: Determine Requirements

The decision on working capital technology begins with an analysis of a company's requirements, particularly considering how data is currently used and whether there are any perceived deficiencies. Management should focus on situations where information is clearly inadequate to support decision making. For example, which products are profitable by customer and by market? Would this information assist us in making better decisions, or is it interesting but not particularly critical? And, can it be developed from existing data sources?

A useful approach is to establish an ad hoc project team to compile a list of unanswered questions that are important to your business. This committee should represent functions likely to be affected by any decision on a new system. The list should drive the decision on whether to proceed to Phase 2. Here are a few concerns noted by companies in recent technology reviews.

---

8. See "CHAOS Summary 2009" (April 23, 2009), at standishgroup.com/newsroom/chaos_2009.php. This conclusion was supported by academic research reported in H. Liang, N. Saraf, Q. Hu and Y. Xue, "Assimilation of Enterprise Systems: The Effect of Institutional Pressures and the Mediating Role of Top Management," *MIS Quarterly* 31 (2007), pp. 59–87.

- What time of day does the company typically know its cash position? Is this timing adequate to allow finance to make optimal investing or borrowing decisions?

- Are interfaces to accounting, financial, and other systems primarily manual, involving internal company communications and the rekeying of data? Does this situation cause difficulties in managing our business or an unacceptable error rate, or is it merely an inconvenience?

- Do we use just-in-time (see Chapter 6) and are we sufficiently knowledgeable about the financial health of our vendors? What would happen if there were a bankruptcy or a serious shipping delay?

- What is our customer retention history? Do we attempt to sell "up" to our more profitable customers, or is our marketing primarily reactive to incoming opportunities?

- Do our employees understand the strategy for expanding our business? Would better training, selection practices, and/or compensation improve our ability to deliver quality products or services to the marketplace?

- Would a function-specific application be adequate for our requirements? For example, can we make do with a foreign exchange and investment quotation system (e.g., Bloomberg), a system that supports specific assets or liabilities, or a risk-management system (see Chapter 10)?

Phase 2: Conduct Vendor Search

Venues that provide competitive information on bank and ERP products include the following:

- *Bank technology conferences.* The most important exhibition for banks and vendors is the Association of Financial Professionals

(AFP) annual conference, which meets every autumn in a major U.S. city. There are about 200 exhibitors at this event, perhaps one-third of which offer some form of bank technology. In addition, local treasury associations hold regular meetings. For further information, see www.afponline.org.

- *ERP conferences and seminars.* As with most systems products, conferences and seminars tend to be either sponsored by the vendor (i.e., Microsoft) or by a vendor's users group, or for a specific industry (i.e., retailing). For a partial listing of meetings, see http://panorama-consulting.com/resource-center/events. Some universities teach courses on ERP; for example, the Missouri University of Science and Technology offers programs in conjunction with SAP covering various ERP topics.[9] For current practice on attending conferences and other meetings, see *Tips and Techniques: Technology Demonstrations—Travel or Stay Home?*

- *Web sites and bank contacts.* Your banker and ERP salespeople can arrange for product demonstrations. See Appendix C for a listing of web sites.

TIPS AND TECHNIQUES

Technology Demonstrations— Travel or Stay Home?

The cost of attendance at a national conference that offers opportunities for bank demonstrations of Internet systems can be $4,000 or more, including registration fees, hotel, meals, and transportation. The opportunity to see and compare systems in one central venue was cost effective until the credit crisis that

---

9. See the University's website at http://ist.mst.edu/graduateprograms/ERP.html.

began in 2008. The resulting reduction in staff at many companies, restrictions on travel, and advances in teleconferencing and web site demonstrations now make the in-office review and analysis of competing systems quite feasible.[a]

---

[a]For example, visit JPMorgan Chase at www.jpmorgan.com/cm (treasury services tab) to register for a demonstration and explanation of their electronic banking products. Other bank web sites with similar capabilities are listed in Appendix C.

Banks and vendors should be contacted for detailed information on technology offerings, including modules, hardware requirements, implementation support, and typical pricing. The responses should be reviewed for compatibility with your requirements, and a ranking should be developed to focus on no more than three or four candidate systems. An early recommended step is to request and contact references of companies that are comparable to you in size and industry coverage. See Chapter 4 for more information on the process of reviewing bank and vendor proposals.

Phase 3: Provide Justification to Senior Management

Company's requirements should be matched against the technology specifications provided by bidders. However, traditional economic analysis will not be of much assistance in making the decision on working capital information software. There are three important benefits from such a system that are difficult to subject to traditional capital budgeting analysis:

1. *The quality of the information.* Rather than receiving (or searching for) raw data, working capital managers have the opportunity to view a variety of data organized through logical analysis and reporting.

2. *The opportunity for rationalization of documents and processes.* Bank technology and ERP systems organize existing files from various sources, making it possible to quickly locate actionable information leading to the choice of appropriate business tactics.

3. *The general business process efficiencies gained through the improvement of existing practices.* The reengineering of established but somewhat out-of-date procedures is a major benefit from the decision to implement new working capital technology.

If the decision is based solely on economics, the likelihood is that bank technology will be chosen. In most situations, ERP can only be justified if the time and cost to implement supports the long-term strategy of the company. Whatever decision is made, the following issues should be addressed in the justification statement:

- Which provider will service and maintain the product: the bank, the vendor, the ASP, or internally (probably through the information technology function)? Will the service be available 24/7 or only during normal business hours? Is the product supported by technology experts or by customer service staff who respond to questions?

- What happens in the event of a system failure or disaster? Does the service provider have adequate, secure backup facilities?

- Is there concern for compatibility with other financial and accounting systems?

- Is the product user-friendly or is extensive training required?

- What is the commitment of the bank or vendor to the business? How long is the provider likely to continue to offer support and improve the product?

Tips and Techniques: Information Principles provides additional ideas when evaluating changes in technology

Information Principles

When considering information changes in support of working capital management, consider seven basic principles to guide your decision making.

1 Remember that technology is not magic, nor is it an end; it is a means (a tool) to the end.

2 Define the purpose of the working capital function.

3 Determine the functions and proper use of people, process, and technology.

4 Use a disciplined methodology to create and reengineer your workplace.

5 Learn how to exploit the functionalities of bank or ERP systems.

6 Analyze the costs and benefits of information systems as rigorously as any capital budgeting decision.

7 Assure that there is security, privacy, and regulatory compliance.

Summary

Information technology decisions require the analysis of several issues: Are our requirements likely to be met, is there adequate internal support, do we fully understand the necessary investment, and have we considered using an outsourcing vendor (such as an application service provider)? The two primary choices are bank information technology and an enterprise resource planning systems, and decision factors include cost, ease of access, comprehensiveness of the module offerings, the opportunity to redesign internal processes, and the extent of future internal commitment to manage these resources. A three-phase process is recommended to resolve these issues:

1. Determine requirements.

2. Conduct a vendor search.

3. Provide justification to senior management.

CHAPTER 10

Managing the Working Capital Cycle

After reading this chapter, you will be able to:

- Understand risk management issues in working capital including enterprise risk management.

- Appreciate the measurement of working capital efficiency.

- Determine how liquidity is managed.

- Consider how traditional and modern attitudes have changed the management of working capital.

- Review working capital ideas and implementation procedures.

Throughout this book we have discussed the accounts on the balance sheet that drive working capital, including current assets and liabilities. In addition, we devoted chapters to international and information systems issues. There are three concerns in managing the working capital cycle that encompass essential topics in managing any business: risk management, efficiency, and liquidity. Each will be discussed in this chapter.

Risk and Working Capital

Risk is in the possibility of loss or injury. Until recently, the measurement of risk has been through the frequency of human or property loss in specific categories, such as death or disability by age, sex, and occupation, or the frequency of fire damage to specific types of construction at various locations. In the past, we managed risk using established hedging mechanisms, including insurance, futures, and options; see Chapter 6.

With an insurance policy, the policyholder accepts a small certain loss—the premium expense—rather than the possibility of a large catastrophic loss. Futures and options are types of derivative contracts traded on exchanges that guarantee a price for a specified later time. The buyer of the contract is under no obligation to take delivery and may terminate the contract by selling (closing) the position or letting it lapse without taking action.[1]

Risks Inherent in Working Capital

Markets now recognize that there are types of working capital risk that require management action even though there are no established hedges to mitigate these events.

- *Operational risk* is normal to business as it arises from problems with technology, employees, or operations. These risks are often managed by the establishment of policies and procedures to govern the conduct of ongoing activities. Realistically, behaviors cannot be regulated by proclamation. However, assigning specific duties states the company's position on responsibilities, sets a charter for acceptable corporate and employee behavior, and assesses penalties should violations occur.

---

1. A *forward* is similar to a futures contract, but differs in that it is a private agreement in which no exchange or clearinghouse participates. Forwards are almost entirely used for foreign exchange transactions. We discussed forwards in Chapter 8.

- *Credit risk* concerns the failure of customers to pay amounts owed and due in a timely manner. We manage these types of risk through credit reports and debt management services provided by credit reporting companies; see Chapter 5 for a discussion.

- *Liquidity risk* is a company's inability to pay obligations as they come due, resulting in financial embarrassment, a negative impact on the company's credit rating and vendor relations, and potential bankruptcy. This risk is managed by arranging for lines of credit and access to other "safety" financing; see Chapter 3.

- *Information-reporting risk* is the receipt of inaccurate information from a financial institution or vendor, usually in the daily transmission of bank account entries, balances, or transactions. These errors can result from formatting errors or from misunderstandings as to the meaning of specific data fields. This risk is managed by carefully matching book (ledger) entries to bank or vendor entries, and immediately reconciling any variances by communications with the reporter of the information; see Chapter 9.

Conventional Risk Management

In the past, the administration of risk has been through separate business functions, the responsibilities for which reside with various organizational units. When risks are treated in this manner, internal specialists have managed risks as independent activities. For example:

- Lawyers and compliance officers treat regulatory and political risks.

- Insurance buyers acquire coverage for various types of life and health, and property and casualty risks.

- Security specialists, occupational safety and health advisors, environmental engineers, and contingency and crisis management planners all work individually toward a safe and secure work environment.

- Financial staff manages derivative, liquidity, foreign exchange, interest rate, and financial institution risks.

- Credit and collection or account receivable monitors credit risk.

Using this approach, the interdependencies and interrelationships of business risks can be overlooked, resulting in potentially inadequate safeguards for the assets of the organization.

Enterprise Risk Management

Enterprise risk management (ERM) attempts to identify, prioritize, and quantify the risks from all sources that threaten the working capital and strategic objectives of the corporation. The ERM approach views risk as pervasive in a company and considers a coordinated approach through a formal administrative function to be essential. ERM reduces the volatility inherent in business activities and helps to achieve consistent earnings and manage costs. Adverse business and financial incidents have occurred in various industries, such as the Exxon oil spill in 1989,[2] the Ford/Bridgestone-Firestone tire recall crisis in 2000,[3] and the Toyota accelerator problem in 2010.

One popular approach to ERM has been *Value at Risk* (VaR). VaR is an approach to determining the risk exposure in a portfolio of assets. Although certain risks (e.g., financial instruments, credit, commodity prices) can be forced into the VaR model, it is a process that is heavily dependent on historical patterns. Other risks are not subject to the same statistical calculations and may be inadequately considered. Some

---

2. A tanker belonging to the Exxon Corporation—the *Exxon Valdez*—ran aground in the Prince William Sound in Alaska, spilling millions of gallons of crude oil into the waters off Valdez. As a result, thousands of fish, fowl, and sea otters died; miles of coastline were polluted; salmon spawning runs were disrupted; and groups of fishermen, especially Native Americans, lost their livelihoods. The extent and resolution of the disaster from the BP oil rig explosion and leakage in the Gulf of Mexico in 2010 is unresolved as this book goes to press.
3. Bridgestone/Firestone recalled 6.5 million tires in response to claims that their 15-inch Wilderness AT, radial ATX and ATX II tire treads were separating from the tire core, leading to a series of deadly crashes. These tires were mostly used on the Ford Explorer, the world's top-selling sport utility vehicle (SUV).

companies using VaR supplement their analysis by stress testing to determine likely performance in various worst-case scenarios.

VaR calculates the amount of risk inherent in a financial portfolio with a predefined confidence level (usually 95 percent), including risk covariance.[4] Computer model simulations typically cannot anticipate the "perfect storm" (or worst-case) scenario, when all factors are adverse at the same time. The latter can occur when markets are illiquid (as in 2008–2009).

ERM Process

ERM involves separate steps that should be supported by a continuous monitoring process.

- *Identifying risk.* The first step is to scan or recognize the elements of a company's working capital risks. Although various types of risk were noted earlier, every organization faces a unique set of variables that must be specified and enumerated.

- *Measuring and prioritizing risk.* Not all risks should be proactively managed, and managers should prioritize and act on those with potential significance to the security of the business. High-priority working capital risks could include the following:

  - A marketing decision that could impact a product or a customer relationship.

  - Significant problems with critical information systems.

  - Substantial increases in cost factors.

  - Sudden cash outflows due to unexpected expenses.

  - Suppliers and/or customer defaults.

---

4. *Covariance* is the measure of how much two random variables vary together; that is, if an independent event were to occur (such as a fire in one location), what is the likelihood that another independent event will occur (such as a flood in a different location).

Medium-priority risks would include any action that could impact the goals in the business plan but do not threaten the company. Examples could include problems with noncritical information systems and the loss of a significant customer or of a contract.

- *Managing enterprise risk.* The company must determine the likely occurrence of each risk not yet subject to conventional risk management techniques, the application of outcome probabilities, the determination of the covariance of risk dependencies, and the development of appropriate actions.

Efficiency and Working Capital

The ratios developed in earlier chapters are insufficient to absolutely determine evidence of good or poor working capital management. Using Troy's metrics (denoted as "Selected Financial Ratios"), which were referenced in Chapter 1, we see that the Rengas Company we've been examining is producing superior profitability compared to its industry (plastics manufacturing); see Exhibit 10.1. Additional evidence in Exhibit 10.2 seems to imply that Rengas appears to be doing an

---

EXHIBIT 10.1

Financial Ratios

	Industry Mean	Rengas Company
Current ratio	1.5 times	2.9 times
Quick ratio	0.8 times	2.2 times
Receivables turnover	7.4 times	5.5 times
Inventory turnover	7.2 times	6.7 times
Profits to sales	1.5%	9.1%
Return on equity	7.9%	21.8%

Sources: Industry ratios are based on Leo Troy, *Almanac of Business and Industrial Financial Ratios* (New York: Commerce Clearing House, 2006; 2009); company ratios are derived from the Exhibits 1.1 and 1.2 financial statements.

EXHIBIT 10.2

Supplemental Ratios

(times)	Industry Mean	Rengas Company
Net sales to WC	10.0	3.5
Current assets to WC	3.0	1.5
Current liabilities to WC	2.0	0.5
Total receipts to cash flow*	9.1	30.0
CGS to cash flow*	6.6	20.0

WC = working capital

*Troy defines cash flow as the difference between cash receipts and cash disbursements. For purposes of this analysis, the net cash position in Exhibit 1.1 is used in Exhibit 10.2.

Sources: Industry ratios are based on Leo Troy, *Almanac of Business and Industrial Financial Ratios* (New York: Commerce Clearing House, 2006; 2009); company ratios are derived from the Exhibits 1.1 and 1.2 financial statements.

excellent job in managing cash and other working capital components. Let's look a little deeper.

Management Differences in Current Asset Accounts

As we discussed in Chapter 1 (in the traditional and modern views of working capital), excessive working capital constitutes a hindrance to performance. Emphasis should be on reducing these requirements so that current liabilities can be funded from the ongoing operations of a business. Close examination of our illustrative company shows that both current assets and current liabilities are excessive, and that receivables and inventory are underperforming versus the industry.

These findings are summarized in the current and quick ratios, both of which are superior in the traditional view but mediocre in the modern view of working capital. More aggressive management of accounts receivable to the industry average would reduce that current asset to about $20 million (from $27.5 million), and of inventory would reduce that account to about $14 million (from $15 million). The total savings would be about $8.5 million.

It is somewhat ironic that the cash portion of the working capital cycle in our example shows superior performance but the receivables and inventory portions are underperforming. The urgency of access to cash has led to various banking products that have improved cash management (see Chapter 2), while focus on other working capital elements has lagged. Banks began to develop these services in the 1970s when short-term interest rates rose to nearly 20 percent. Companies gradually became educated in their use and advantages, and financial institutions found that attractive returns and corporate client "capture" resulted from aggressive promotion of suites of cash products.

There has not been a similar effort in inventory, receivables, or payables management, and in fact, materials suppliers and customers demonstrate behaviors that often lead to poor management. For example, if your company has acquired unsalable inventory or materials that have decayed, the natural response is to buy replacements and scrap or warehouse the unusable portion. In effect, the problem continues and may even become worse, and gets attention only one time a year when a physical inventory is taken for purposes of financial reporting. Similarly, slow and no paying customers are carried beyond any reasonable time, because it is easier to sell to existing customers than find new buyers.

Required Teamwork

Opportunities to reduce total working capital cycle time must be investigated by the appropriate disciplines:

- The materials element requires input from the purchasing function.
- The work-in-process element should be examined by production managers.
- Invoice preparation needs attention from production, invoicing, and information technology managers.
- Receipt of funds includes elements of receivables management, finance, and credit and collection, and requires input from these areas.

The development of data from these various functions demands more teamwork than is customary in many traditional line-and-staff organizations; recall our earlier comments regarding organizing for each working capital element. Lack of cooperation is often the cause of failure when results are below industry averages. The recommended integrative approach can be used both to plan the pricing and profitability of products and services, and to determine the cause of failure to meet profitability targets.[5]

Liquidity and Working Capital

The examination of recent data on liquidity shows that the current ratio of American businesses has barely changed in the past three years, while the cash required to support sales activity has declined in every observation selected from a sample representing 20 percent of U.S. industries; see Exhibit 10.3.[6] Stability in the current ratio and the resulting minimal information content reflects the re-alignment of working capital by companies to changing economic conditions.

How to Measure and Manage Liquidity

A much more useful measure is total receipts (revenues for most companies) to cash flow (TR/CF). Between 2005 and 2008, TR/CF declined from 9.8 times to 6.8 times.[7] Applying these revenue data to the ratio of receipts to cash flow, we note that cash rose from 10.2 to 15.4 percent of

---

5. For a complete discussion of these concepts, see James Sagner, *Financial and Process Metrics for the New Economy*, (New York: AMACOM Books, 2001).

6. This section is based on James Sagner, "How to Measure and Manage Liquidity Today," *Journal of Corporate Accounting and Finance*, Nov/Dec 2009, pp. 47–50.

7. Based on calculations by the author from a sample of Current Ratios (#30) and ratios of Total Receipts to Total Cash Flow (#42) for 25 industries (of about 135 industries); Leo Troy, *Almanac of Business and Industrial Ratios* (New York: CCH, 2006; 2009), Table 1: Companies with and without Net Income. Excluded from the sample were public utilities (as revenues are regulated by public service commissions), financial companies, and professional service organizations.

EXHIBIT 10.3

Changes in Liquidity Ratios in U.S. Industry Groups (2006–2009)[a]

Industry Groups	NAICS Series[b]	Change in Current Ratio	Change in Total Receipts to Cashflow
Agriculture	11	0.17	−0.23
Mining	21	−0.25	−0.40
Construction	23	0.08	−0.29
Manufacturing	31–33	0.01	−0.41
Wholesaling	42	0.00	−0.29
Retailing	44–45	−0.03	−0.15
Transportation and Warehousing	48–49	0.13	−0.20
Information	51	−0.02	−0.38
Other	62–72	0.11	−0.12
Unweighted Change[c]		*0.02*	*−0.30*

[a] The period representing the top of the economic cycle to the present time.

[b] For a complete listing of all North American Industry Classification System (NAICS) codes, see www.naics.com.

[c] Calculated based on the individual changes in 25 industries.

Source: Based on calculations by the author from a sample of current ratios (#30) and ratios of total receipts to total cash flow (#42) for 25 industries (of about 135 industries); Leo Troy, *Almanac of Business and Industrial Ratios* (Commerce Clearing House, 2006; 2009), Table 1: Companies with and without Net Income. Excluded from the sample were public utilities (as revenues are regulated by public service commissions), and financial companies and professional service organizations.

the balance sheets of the companies in this sample,[8] an increase of more than one-third in only three years. This reflects the rapidly declining reliance of businesses on short-term credit lines from banks and other sources, and the hoarding of cash to meet transactional and precautionary needs. By 2009, the amount of cash had fallen to 13.4 percent, indicative of improved bank credit line lending and a gradually improving economy.

---

8. Calculated as TR/CF, or for every $100 of revenue in 2005 there was $9.80 of cash, equal to 10.2%, and for every $100 of inflation-adjusted revenue ($104.75) there was $6.80 of cash in 2008, equal to 15.4% in 2008. By 2009 with generally improved economic conditions, the percentage of cash of total assets was 13.4%, or for every inflation-adjusted $100 of revenue ($106.50) of revenue in 2009, there was $7.94 of cash.

These data support our previous conclusion that many businesses have become knowledgeable and aggressive in managing their cash positions.

- *Adjustment by business.* Companies have adjusted remarkably well to the 2008–2010 contraction of credit and liquidity, and to weakened economic conditions. Certainly there have been companies that failed to adequately cope with these unprecedented conditions (at least since the Great Depression), and the result has been bankruptcy. However, many businesses have taken the necessary steps to survive, such as terminating marginal employees, negotiating with vendors and landlords, and working harder and smarter.

- *Need for new liquidity measurements.* The traditional tools for measuring liquidity are not helpful in the current situation. The underlying assumptions in using these techniques are predictable revenues and costs, and available credit at a fair price to worthy borrowers. As businesspeople know only too well, in recent times revenues have not been predictable and credit remains tight.

  Instead, liquidity needs must be calculated from longer-term results, by industry, using data from Troy on total receipts to cash flow. Banks are taking note of this situation, and future loan covenants (as discussed in Chapter 3) may stress TR/CF over the less useful standard liquidity ratios as protection against providing credit in deteriorating business conditions.

- *The appropriate amount of liquidity.* Cash is only a portion of the liquidity requirements of any business. The typical U.S. company should carry about 10 percent of its balance sheet (measured as total assets) as cash in normal times, assuming an additional 5 percent of liquidity will be available from bank credit lines. In times of economic distress such as 2008–2009, cash holdings rise to about 15 percent of the balance sheet. Inevitably, higher cash holdings result in lessened expenditures for current assets and capital project investments, and will stifle growth and profitability.[9] However, the priority in a credit crisis must be survival rather than long-term strategic concerns.

- *An integrated approach to managing other working capital accounts.* Cash is only one portion of a comprehensive working capital effort; receivables, inventory, and payables are collectively more significant in money terms and deserve equivalent attention.

Suggested Actions

Here are 50 action steps that businesses should be taking to assure survival and eventual growth. Measuring and understanding working capital requirements are essential components of any company's financial plan. For implementation ideas, see *Tips and Techniques: Changes to Working Capital Management—How to Get Started.*

General Ideas

1. Calculate the cost of capital to value the savings that may be available in reducing working capital.

2. Determine the amount of working capital float and consider alternative processes to improve float management.

3. Use ratio analysis to compare working capital performance against industry averages.

4. Understand that cash is found in three forms—bank cash, line of credit cash, and cash invested short-term—and each must be individually managed for optimal results.

---

9. A 2010 study by Thomson Reuters concludes that the top 50 companies in the United States hold nearly $500 billion in cash! Reported by Michael J. de la Merced, "Flush and Looking to Spend," *New York Times*, Apr. 1, 2010, p. F2.

TIPS AND TECHNIQUES

Changes to Working Capital Management—How to Get Started

Any attempt at a comprehensive working capital effort will seem daunting when management is faced with the variety and quantity of issues developed in this book. A useful approach may be to assign specific sets of tasks to ad hoc committees comprised of representatives of each functional area likely to be affected. The list could be organized by working capital account. However, you may choose to use a different allocation of assignments, such as by the oldest or newest information system affected by the idea, or by the extent of the effort necessary to effectuate change (from heroic through minor).

The next step is to determine current practice—the "base" case. Documentation of that status assists in deciding whether change is necessary and feasible, and eventually how much the change will cost. Each committee should issue a report showing: A brief description of the working capital change, how the system currently works, which functions are responsible, whether information technology or vendor interfaces will be affected, the cost and benefits from the change, any additional data that is required, and the time required for implementation. Senior management can then prioritize company working capital change efforts.

5. Forecast short-term business activity; consider the distribution method or another statistical technique.

6. Develop a cash budget capability and maintain updates at appropriate frequencies.

7. Review risk management techniques for elements of working capital.

Banking Ideas

8. Examine bank products for possible application to the management of float and prevention fraud.

9. Determine the appropriateness of your company's bank account structure. What is the cost and purpose of each account, and who are the authorized signers?

10. Review procedures used to mobilize funds in depository (collection) account(s) for transfer to your concentration account(s) and disbursement account(s).

11. Arrange for a line of credit at your bank to cover temporary cash deficiencies.

12. Consider financing your working capital through an asset-based lending facility.

13. Drain any excess funds from bank accounts where only a minimal earnings credit rate is received.

14. Invest temporary excess cash through an appropriate short-term instrument.

15. Write policies for short-term investments.

16. Develop long-term bank relationship(s) including credit and non-credit services.

17. Consider using a request for proposal to bid (or rebid) banking services.

Receivables Ideas

18. Develop appropriate policies and focus your company on the management of receivables.

19. Review and take appropriate action on your receivables aging schedule.

20. Consider using sales financing to assist customers to purchase your products. If sales financing is currently used, review the terms of these credit deals to ascertain that your company is receiving a fair return.

21. Use a credit reporting service to assist in decisions on accepting or rejecting new customers.

22. Review your terms of sale, possibly adding or changing any cash or other discounts offered.

23. Analyze the entire process of generating invoices, including design and timing.

24. Use a debt collection agency to pursue slow and nonpaying customers.

Inventory Ideas

25. Develop appropriate policies and focus your company on the management of inventory.

26. Examine the purchasing cycle and determine if it is in compliance with appropriate procedures.

27. Determine if there are specific purchasing problem areas such as high prices paid, or lack of compliance with PO and receiving report requirements.

28. Calculate your EOQ for each significant purchase and determine optimal procedures.

29. Consider whether JIT is appropriate and any possible risks.

30. Examine supply chain management systems for adaptation to your company.

Payables Ideas

31. Develop appropriate policies and focus your company on the management of payables.

32. Actively manage accounts payable and determine when to release payments.

33. Review the terms of sale offered by vendors, possibly taking any cash or other discounts offered.

34. Consider alternatives to check disbursements for vendors, such as procurement cards, freight and logistics services, and comprehensive payables.

35. Evaluate alternatives to payroll checks including direct deposit and paycard.

International Ideas

36. Establish an international working capital committee to monitor current asset and liability activities and to provide input to local managers on appropriate policy.

37. Review policies on corporate governance and work toward transparency and reporting on the behavior of your company in global markets.

38. Manage foreign exchange transaction exposure using forward contracts.

39. Request letters of credit to manage credit risks from international sales. Review LC activity and consider using banks with electronic LC services.

40. Consider establishing multicurrency accounts to manage FX.

41. Begin moving international transactions to any of several electronic mechanisms in order to eliminate paper checks.

42. Review business risk in international markets using country risk assessment services.

43. Consider the potential advantages of tax-advantaged or reinvoicing centers to manage regional activity in global markets.

44. Be aware of different cultural and corporate practices in international working capital.

Information Technology Ideas

45. Review existing and/or proposed information technology to determine that current and future requirements of your company are addressed. Ascertain if a comprehensive approach (e.g., ERP) is better than limited improvements to existing systems as supplemented by bank technology.

46. Determine if an information project has an internal champion or whether the idea came from senior management or a vendor who has possibly lost interest.

47. Fully analyze all acquisition and implementation expenses to determine the project's economic viability, and consider whether an ASP might be a more cost-effective solution.

Ideas on Managing the Working Capital Cycle

48. Analyze the business risks facing your company. Determine if ERM may be appropriate as a comprehensive risk management program.

49. Review the efficiency with which working capital is managed. Efforts to reduce the total working capital cycle time require a cooperative effort by appropriate business disciplines.

50. Manage the liquidity requirements of your company to meet current and potential demands for access to cash regardless of the business environment. Once the current economic crisis has passed, prepare to reduce cash and to resume aggressive actions to minimize your investment in working capital.

Developments in Working Capital Management

There have been important changes to the economic structure of entire industries in the past few decades as business has become global, technology has affected decision making and communications, and finance has offered new challenges and opportunities.

Twentieth-Century Business Model

Traditional business strategies required holding current as well as fixed assets on the balance sheet to create differentiated manufacturing, technology, and marketing processes. Few competitors could match an established company's blend of product offerings and distribution channels, and this special market position generated oligopolistic profits.[10] Industries could continue in their protected status for years, confident that any disruptions could be fixed and that a challenge by an upstart could be met.

The vertically integrated twentieth-century manufacturing company often dominated an entire economic sector. Businesses like General Motors owned sources of raw materials, converted that inventory to finished goods, controlled distribution channels, and only dealt with vendors when special products were required for a continuous manufacturing flow, for example, automobile and truck tires. Vendors, auto dealers, and even customers were their captives, and the accumulation of current and fixed assets was critical to the perpetuation of this position.

Twenty-First-Century Business Model

Best Buy (discussed in Chapter 1) and similar companies have introduced a different business model—one where results are based on minimum working capital, tight control over costs, low profits per transaction, very high sales turnover, and fewer owned assets. An important element is the development of strategic relationships between businesses and their vendors.

In thinking about working capital specifically, and finance in general, a useful concept is the cash-flow timeline, shown as Exhibit 10.4.

---

10. An oligopoly is a form of industrial concentration where there are several large companies, any one of which can affect the price and product features offered.

EXHIBIT 10.4

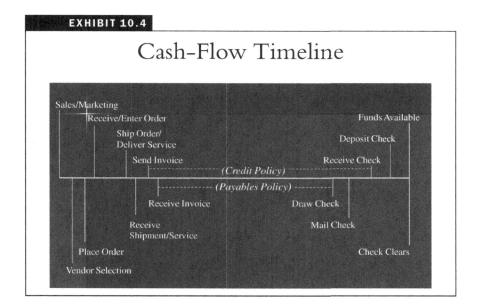

The horizontal axis represents time, and each activity along the timeline—note how many there are—requires the commitment of days for completion. A typical transaction cycle in business can involve 90 or 120 days from the purchase of raw materials through the receipt of funds from the customer.

The Cost of a Transaction

The aggregated time for a transaction may require weeks or months, with each segment having a financial value or cost, identified as float, as measured by the transaction dollars being managed times the cost of capital times the time period (measured as the percentage of a year). For example, assume a $50,000 transaction requiring three and a half months. If the cost of capital is 10 percent, there is nearly $1,500 in the cost of float, calculated as $50,000 \times 3.5/12 \times 10$ percent. And this is just one transaction cycle of possibly thousands in a year of activity!

To optimize the cash-flow timeline, financial managers must encourage their staff to adopt a consultative attitude, seeking areas within the company for application of financial knowledge. Cash and information are the critical elements, because each step in the operation of a business involves decisions that impact both resources. The issue of time (float) can vitally affect profitability; for an example, see *In the Real World: How Delays Turn Forecast Profits into Actual Losses.*

IN THE REAL WORLD

How Delays Turn Forecast Profits into Actual Losses

In a typical situation, you plan profits so that your returns exceed costs; in capital budgeting terms, your internal rate of return (IRR) exceeds your financing costs. Fine—you've met the threshold requirement. Or have you? While you think you're experiencing a small ledger profit, you may really be receiving a minimal return when adjusted for the cost of capital (in other words, the float).

Let's take a live example. Your customer wants 200 gross gizmos on which you target a 10 percent margin (profit). However, the customer wants some concessions:

- A 4 percent price discount—a sales issue.
- Delivery to particular quality standards—a manufacturing or engineering issue.
- Billing 30 days after delivery—a credit or accounts receivable issue.
- An advertising rebate—a marketing issue.
- A check that will take two days to clear that will be sent 40 days after invoicing—a treasury issue.

Why do we bother to cite the functions responsible? These decisions take time and cooperation among various internal organizations, which was acceptable in the twentieth century but not in the competitive business climate of the twenty-first century.

Should we accept or decline the gizmo deal? In the past you had weeks to decide. In that time, you could ponder the situation, consult your accountants or old records; talk to your priest, rabbi or bartender; or negotiate a better deal with the customer. Competitive pressures today give you hours or possibly minutes to decide. You will make many bad decisions unless you can calculate the number of days required to perform each element in the working capital cycle. In fact, there is a strong likelihood of large, established, mostly traditional companies facing a potentially disastrous series of transaction losses.

Here are summarized financial calculations. The target margin per gross is $500. The ledger actual margin is $67, due to a sales discount on the standard price and various additional cost elements. However, when float is considered, the return is actually −$17. This is primarily due to delays in receiving payment for the sale, alleviated to a very slight extent by delays in paying for the costs associated with the sale. All of the elements of the cash-flow timeline affect profitability. In the gizmo deal, 10 of 25 manufacturing elements contributed and all of the administrative elements contributed to the profitability problem, with no single element responsible.

Here are our choices:

- Negotiate with our customer.
- Improve our internal operations.
- Decline the deal.

How These Situations Can Occur

In three decades of working with global Fortune 1000 companies, we have seen countless situations of inefficiencies and inappropriate financial practices in these "nonfinancial" business functions. Many organizations permit managers, supervisors and even clerks to have some financial authority without either the specific delegated responsibility or an understanding of important financial concepts.

Such decisions often occur on the spur of the moment in order to move a transaction along to its completion. However, success for the function—such as closing a sale—may actually be a mediocre result for the organization if the financial component of the deal is a nominal gain or a loss. Estimates of financial inefficiencies in U.S. businesses are in the billions of dollars annually. Clearly, the profession must actively pursue opportunities to improve business processes and restore competitive performance.

Interconnectivity in the Twenty-First Century

Companies in the twenty-first century will continue to focus on business activity groupings that optimize the only resources that cross all organizational functions: cash and information. And financial managers must begin to accept the idea—regardless of functional domicile—that they are their enterprises' experts for managing its working capital and other financial assets. Furthermore, this focus must transcend your company's boundaries and optimize operations with suppliers and customers.

- Suppliers will become partners in managing working capital because they will hold inventory until just prior to its use and will provide a level of quality that allows materials to immediately enter into a production process.
- Customers will be partners, as they will be expected to pay for goods and services at a time nearer to when they place orders (the business model used by Dell Computer) or when the merchandise is purchased (the Best Buy model).

If suppliers and customers cannot accept these conditions, then a hard choice must be made as to whether they should be in the relationship. But note: This must be a partnership and not an ongoing conflict between adversaries. What a revolutionary idea!

Summary

The three enterprise concerns in managing the working capital cycle are risk management, efficiency, and liquidity. Working capital risks include operational, credit, liquidity and information reporting, and enterprise risk management systems attempt to provide comprehensive risk solutions. Efficiency and liquidity issues relate to the interrelationship of cash-flow timeline elements and the need to focus greater management emphasis on receivables, inventory, and payables.

Suggested Solutions to Widget Manufacturing Company Case— Parts I, II, and III

Part I

Solution 1: The first step in helping Arnold is to calculate the ratios that will be important in identifying the problems at Widget.

	Widget	Industry
Liquidity Ratios		
Current ratio	2.33	2.75
Quick ratio	1.03	1.63
Receivables turnover	4.28	7.72
Average collection period (days)	84.16	47.48
Other Ratios		
Asset turnover	1.12	1.96
Inventory turnover	2.40	7.02
Return on equity	0.04	25.95

The results clearly show that Widget is below all of the industry's averages and not from managing working capital in a modern (versus traditional) manner. There really are no exceptions, especially with Widget now forced to come to terms with problems throughout the business. It is astonishing that Arnold was able to convince I. M. Cash to go along with him on providing financing over the years; he and I. M. must have pulled some interesting pranks in high school! However, I. M. did not do Arnold any favors; he was the person who should have warned Arnold about poor management decisions beginning years ago.

Solution 2: Arnold should be looking for the correct level of net working capital and how he will finance it.

- Inventories are turning around three times slower than the industry average, indicating that the firm probably has either excess or stale inventory. Regardless of the cause, Widget has too much capital tied up in inventory that is not earning a reasonable return per dollar invested.

- Accounts receivable are similarly out of line, turning at just under twice the industry's rate. Although Widget's terms are the same as those of the industry, receivables are much higher indicating that the company could tighten its collection policy without hurting sales.

Month-end reporting of local balances by plant controllers is inadequate for maintaining tight control over cash balances. Although computerized balance reporting systems may not be cost justified for the smaller banks, daily or weekly telephone calls may be appropriate. Excess or deficit cash positions should be handled via ACH or Fedwire funds transfers rather than paper checks. Balance management would become much more controllable if collections are moved to lockboxes at a single site and disbursements are done through a single bank.

More timely and improved cash forecasting processes would permit more aggressive short-term investment management, yielding better returns than those available through overnight repos late in the day. It could also minimize the need to borrow from the line of credit at the prime rate +3 percent (a total of 6.25 percent as of April 2010).

Part II

Note: Calculations were developed on the float or cost for a full year and are based on 250 business days.

Solution 3: Without a physical inspection by a qualified expert, it is difficult to judge the condition of the inventory. There is a real possibility that a significant portion is stale and will bring only a small amount of the carrying cost, particularly given the fast obsolescence in the consumer electronics industry. In any event, Arnold's objectives should be to raise cash by attracting buyers to Widget's low prices and to get inventories in line with what is reasonable based on average industry results.

Solution 4: The value of vendors' cash discount is 360 ÷ 30 (derived from 40 "net" days − 10 "discount" days) or 12, × 1.5 percent = 18 percent. This is not sufficiently attractive to be worth taking although likely higher than Widget's cost of capital. Furthermore, if Widget pays all of these invoices in 50 days rather 40 days, the value becomes only 13.5 percent. *Note*: We cannot calculate the cost of capital from the data in the case. However, it could very well be higher than the 10 percent used throughout the book as Widget has numerous operational problems that any good banker (like U. R. Clueless) is certain to spot.

Solution 5: Widget is currently receiving remittances at three plant sites. Without centralizing the processing of receivables, each business unit must maintain a receivables capability. There is no reason these sites couldn't be located at only one location, possibly a bank lockbox. While we cannot determine the optimal site without further analysis, it is nearly certain that a lockbox bank in Chicago—generally acknowledged as the first or second fastest mail city in the United States (along with Atlanta)—would be a reasonable choice. The first step is to centralize

collections and close local bank accounts. The potential savings are calculated below.

The four accounts for payables (discussed in the next section) and
collections that can be eliminated are as follows (from Exhibit II.1):

	Average Balance	**Monthly Fees**
Next-to-Last National Bank	$900,000	$6,000
Mediocre National Bank	$1,100,000	$6,000
Epter National Bank of Michigan	$800,000	$7,000
Second National Bank of Chicago—Account B	$600,000	$5,000
Totals	$3,400,000	$24,000

The gross savings from eliminating balances would be $340,000
(calculated as $3.4 million × the 10% cost of capital), and from bank
fees of nearly $290,000 a year ($24,000 × 12 months). In addition, there
would be float savings of probably 2 days through the use of a Chicago
lockbox. The savings are equivalent to about $745,000 a year (calculated
as 2 days × daily sales of $3.73 million [$931.6 million ÷ 250 business
days] × 10%). Assuming an average payment of $20,000, the lockbox
cost would be $50,000 (calculated as 50,000 payments × $1 per lockbox
transaction).

There would also be savings by eliminating the labor intensive function of receiving and depositing collections. The result would be a total
savings of perhaps $1.25 million a year (assuming most payments are
converted to lockbox). In addition, control would be improved in that
Widget employees would not be touching any live checks. The lockbox
and other fees paid to Second National would greatly enhance the Widget banking relationship.

The second step is to develop or outsource a centralized invoicing
system. This action would have the additional advantage of eliminating
redundant Accounts Receivable (A/R) clerks, would place all of the
data about A/R aging by account in one location, and would improve

control over the entire process. The aging schedule (Exhibit II.3) shows that more than 20 percent of receivables are past due ($931.6 million ÷ $217.8 million) with more than 5 percent over 90 days late! This is simply an intolerable situation, and these customers should be told to pay or find another vendor and face legal action.

Local payroll and payables activities create too many bank accounts, too many funding activities, and too expensive disbursement banking system. The costs of the current payroll system are as follows:

	Average Balance	Monthly Fees
Last National Bank of St. Louis	$1,000,000	$6,000
Almost Last National Bank	$1,200,000	$5,000
Inept National Bank of Michigan	$800,000	$7,000
Second National Bank of Chicago—Account A	$600,000	$6,000
Totals	$3,600,000	$24,000

The float value and fees for these accounts is $650,000 ($3.6 million × 10% + $290,000), with net savings of about $600,000 after the cost of direct depositing. Paying the payroll by check from local banks misses the opportunity to directly deposit pay, which would save the cost of managing that portion of the disbursement accounts. If checks are the preferred method of payment, a single account should be used for all payroll to maximize float and to simplify account management. Many of these costs can be reduced by eliminating accounts and using an outsourcing payroll vendor.

Local payables management could cause some early payment of invoices, some missed cash discounts, and failure to negotiate quantity purchase discounts. Because the same clerk is handling both cash and accounting functions, there is a control issue at each company site. The second signature requirement is not an adequate safeguard against fraud as the clerk could issue checks to a phony vendor for any amount under $2,500.

Widget issues 7,500 checks a month for payables at a cost of $5 each. The total cost of this activity is $450,000. If a comprehensive payables bank were used for these payments, the savings would be $360,000 ($450,000 – $90,000 assuming $1 per disbursement). In addition, there would be no control issues with regard to check or electronic payment issuance.

Maintaining an encashment facility at each site not only invites theft but costs the company in lost float. As there are three plant sites and home office handling cash, the total amount of cash is as much as $100,000 at any given time, worth $10,000. An additional cost may be incurred by banks charging for coin and currency services, perhaps another $5,000. The use of this fund for travel and entertainment advances is a control issue in that there may not be adequate documentation provided for each advance. Widget should consider a procurement card for designated managers for such expenses and for small purchases.

In summary, net savings that we calculated are as follows:

Lockboxing/collection system	$1,250,000
Payroll	$600,000
Comprehensive payables	$360,000
Encashment	$15,000
Total	$2,225,000

Furthermore, there are savings opportunities from various other changes, as well as improved control and reduced possibility of fraud.

Solution 6: As discussed in Chapter 3, the sales and expense amounts are accrual accounting estimates and must be converted to cash accounting based on when cash is spent or received. The net cash is added or subtracted from the cash at the beginning of the period and the minimum cash required is deducted from the result. This shows the borrowing required for the period.

The cash budget beginning in June would be as follows:

($ millions)	June	July	August	September	October
Sales	100	120	100	80	60
Collections:					
That month (20%)	20	24	20	16	12
Month after (60%)	48	60	72	60	48
2 months after (20%)	12	16	20	24	20
Total cash in	80	100	112	100	80
Payments:					
Expenses	86	104	86	70	60
Taxes	0	10	0	10	0
Total cash out	86	114	86	80	60
Net cash in/out	−6	−14	26	20	20
Beginning cash	8	2	−12	14	34
Ending cash	2	−12	14	34	54
Minimum cash required	5	5	5	5	5
Surplus/deficit*	−3	−17	9	29	49
Cumulative borrowings**	3	20	11	Repay 18	Repay 49

*Deficit cash is negative and shows required borrowings for any given month.
**For this problem, these borrowings are assumed to begin in June (although we know from the case that Widget had been previously borrowing against its line of credit). "Repay" indicates that these amounts are available to repay earlier borrowings as discussed in Part I of the case.

Solution 7: Based on the calculations in Solution 6, we would borrow $3 million in June and $17 million in July. We would then pay down these borrowings in August in the amount of $9 million and $11 million in September. Although it was not asked in the case, October is shown to indicate that the trend of loan repayment is continuous and positive. Arnold will have to defend these forecasts with names of retailers likely to make purchases and the possible amounts, specific expense data and other projections.

Solution 8: There are so many problems at Widget that it is hard to know where to start. To save the business, Arnold should begin as many of the following changes as possible:

- Have an expert examine inventory and eliminate whatever can be sold, particularly stale inventory.

- Aggressively pursue overdue receivables, even if some customers become offended. They are likely only marginally profitable and are not helping Widget's profits. The aging schedule and the average collection period indicate that Widget really needs to be more aggressive.

- Determine if other assets can be sold and then possibly leased back if essential to Widget's business mission.

- Ignore vendor cash discounts as this would not be a good use of Widget's limited liquidity.

- Advise U. R. Clueless that payments against existing loans can be made in September, later than demanded but certainly substantial in amount. This should give the business a fighting chance to receive an interim loan and to begin to restore the rapport with Second Chicago.

- Work with U. R. Clueless to improve Widget's situation at Second Chicago. Periodic meetings would be useful in improving the relationship.

- Consider raising equity capital. While a sale through the securities markets is unlikely until financial results improve, it may be possible to attract private equity or other sources of funding.

- Begin to work at these changes, and continue to postpone your vacation!

- Consider an outright future sale of the business.

Part III

Solution 9: Arnold has ample reason to be concerned as neither he nor Bernie has experience in international transactions. While peso receipts can be hedged using forwards, there is a cost to these transactions and limited competition in foreign exchange outside of the four major currencies (the U.S. $, the U.K. £, the Japanese ¥, and the €). Furthermore, forwards require a firm transaction date in the future, whereas Mexican and other businesses outside of the United States that may buy from Widget have been known to delay payments for weeks. (There is no FX forwards market for currencies from Central and South America should Widget expand into Latin America.) Arnold could demand a letter of credit for each transaction, but Mexican buyers may choose to do business with a "friendlier" company that has no such requirements.

In addition, Arnold (or Bernie) will have to establish local banking relationships for Mexican peso collections and disbursements. Some receipts will be in pesos and nearly all expenses will be in pesos including local purchases, payroll, taxes, and payments on leased space. Inevitably, mistakes will be made. The complexity of international working capital requires hiring a local treasurer or working capital expert, which will certainly affect the profitability of the planned expansion.

Solution 10: The important working capital issues that Arnold should consider are receivables practices, particularly expectations of when invoices will be paid; inventory management issues in a foreign country, including delivery of essential components; and country risk assessment given the somewhat volatile nature of the Mexican economy. Although the concept of a joint venture (with a Mexican partner) goes beyond the coverage of this book, such an approach may be a viable approach for a fledgling international business.

Joint ventures (JVs) are organized in various formats and ownership shares, with the most common form of structure currently being an international company that partners with a local owner(s). International companies have come to prefer this form of ownership because of the complexity of the culture and the language, the difficulty for foreigners in obtaining approvals and business contacts, the need to keep good managers through an equity incentive, and the tax benefits extended to companies with local participation. However, the loss of control must be considered in any plan to joint venture.

Solution 11: The resolution of these questions is fairly open ended. Widget Manufacturing is clearly in need of a major overhaul of its business functions and staffing. For example, is Bernie the right person to lead the finance function over the next 10 years? Transitioning in a new treasurer could provide an opportunity to consider an ERP system. However, such a radical transformation may be very disruptive to the company and interfere with the many incremental changes so obviously required. For these reasons, and because of the significantly lower cost, bank technology from Second Chicago ("Second Cash") may be the prudent choice for now.

The initial step in deciding on a course of action is described in Chapter 9: "Phase 1: Determine Requirements." An analysis must be made of the company's needs for access to files and records, particularly in consideration of whether there are any glaring deficiencies. The focus should be on situations where information is clearly inadequate to support decision making. Bring the skills and experience of all managers to outline these requirements and determine whether Second Cash (or another product) can begin to formulate an answer.

Basic Financial Concepts

The three financial reports or statements required under accounting rules are the balance sheet, the income statement, and the statement of cash flows. These rules are established by the Financial Accounting Standards Board (FASB), a self-regulating organization managed by the accounting profession, with oversight by the Public Company Accounting Oversight Board (PCAOB) for companies traded on stock exchanges ("public companies"). FASB oversees generally accepted accounting principles (GAAP), which provide accounting standards that are considered as the foundation of financial reporting.

Public companies are required to publish annual reports containing an explanation of the past year's activities, nonconfidential plans for the future, and financial reports including an opinion letter by external auditors as to their accuracy. In addition, public companies must file detailed financial analysis with the primary regulatory agency—the Securities and Exchange Commission (SEC). The annual version of this report is called a 10-K; quarterly reports are known as 10-Qs. Most public companies provide them on their web sites.

General Balance-Sheet Issues

Several issues relate to the entire balance sheet:

- *Date.* All balance sheets are as of a particular date and are valid only for that date. Some businesses use a calendar year reporting period.

However, any date can be used to show financial results, and the period that is used is referred to as the *fiscal year*. As an example, retailers often close the accounting (fiscal) year before or after the Christmas selling season.

- *Asset/liability life.* By convention, the lives of current assets are presumed to be less than one year, while fixed assets are expected to be used by a company and reported on the balance sheet for greater than one year. These assumptions can change at any time and are simply what is expected or known on the balance-sheet date.

- *Listing order.* Assets and liabilities are presented in the order they are likely to be turned into cash, with cash and near-cash items listed first and other items listed later. This characteristic is known as liquidity and is used throughout finance in evaluating investment decisions and calculating capital requirements.

- *Valuation.* All balance-sheet items are valued at the lower cost or market value, which usually means the cost to acquire. Market is used when inventory has lost value due to deterioration, changes in style or other obsolescence, or the loss of a customer for whom the inventory was acquired. This convention is particularly important when a business has owned an asset that has greatly increased in value, such as real estate in New York City, which must be carried at cost and not the current market.

- *Balance.* The left side of the balance sheet—the assets—must equal the right side of the balance—the total of liabilities and net worth. This is accomplished by the procedure of double-entry accounting, with a left-side entry (or a *debit*) equaled by a right-side entry (*credit*) as entries are made to reflect transactions that occur.

- *Notes to financial statements.* The notes that accompany the financial statements may significantly impact the meaning of the data. For example, long-term contractual obligations of the company (such as an operating lease) may only be reported in the notes; yet few investors, lenders, or others who rely on these reports bother to examine the notes.

Assets and Liabilities

As we discussed in Chapter 1, working capital involves current assets and current liabilities. In this section we define noncurrent entries on the balance sheet. The *fixed asset* that is presented in Exhibit 1.1—that is, assets with lives of more than one year—is plant and equipment calculated as plant and equipment at cost less depreciation. The concept of "net" refers to the accounting convention of writing off a portion of the cost of a fixed asset over the estimated life of the asset. In making this calculation, various methods are permitted as selected by management.

These methods are collectively known as "depreciation" and the choice is usually made for tax reasons. Let's assume that the total original cost of the plant and equipment was $100 million. If the life of these assets was estimated to be five years, the company would be allowed to expense $20 million each year ($100 million ÷ 5 years). These assets were apparently owned for two years at the time that the balance sheet was prepared.

There are various conventions used to write down the value of fixed assets. If the company acquires such intangible property as patents, copyrights, or licenses, these assets are subject to *amortization*, which is treatment in the same way as depreciated property. If the company owns natural assets such as oil or gas reserves, coal, or other minerals, this property would be subject to a similar treatment known as *depletion*. Land is presumed to exist forever and is not depreciated or depleted.

The two long-term liabilities will be due in periods beyond one year, and include bonds payable and mortgage payable. *Bonds payable* is debt held by outside investors; *mortgage payable* are loans taken to acquire real property (land and buildings).

Net Worth

Net worth is what the company is worth. The two accounts in net worth are defined as follows:

- *Common stock*. This account represents the total of all monies paid to the company for its stock, including various stock offerings as new stock is sold to investors.

- *Retained earnings*. All of the income (after taxes) remaining in the company (that is, not paid as dividends) are included in retained earnings.

Cost of Capital

Cost of capital is the calculation of the cost to finance a business based on several factors:

- Interest yield on debt.

- Corporate tax rate (as interest is a deductible expense in computing taxable income).

- Dividend yield on equity shares.

- Expected growth in the price of equity shares.

- Weighting of debt and equity on a company's balance sheet.

An illustration is provided below, showing a company that has a 10 percent cost of capital. This is the assumption used throughout this book. However, each business would have to do this calculation based on its own unique situation.

Any investment above this cost should be considered assuming it is consistent with the company's long-term strategy. Any investment returning less than this cost should be rejected as it would negatively affect owner's equity and impair shareholder value. Calculations of returns are a concern of "capital budgeting," which includes such techniques as net present value (NPV) and internal rate of return (IRR).

	Percentage of Balance Sheet	Pre-Tax Cost	After-Tax Cost	Weighted Cost
Debt	40%	7.5% interest yield	5%*	.02
Equity	60%	4% dividend yield + 9.5% growth yield	13.5%	.08
Total Financial Structure	100%			.10

*Calculated as 7.5 % × (1 − corporate tax rate) = 7.5% × the assumed tax rate of 34% = 5%.

An alternative method for the cost of equity capital is the *Capital Asset Pricing Model* (CAPM). In this method, the risk-free return (the rate on U.S. Treasury Bills) is added to the Beta for the company multiplied by the risk premium required by the market for that class of securities. The concepts of Beta and risk premium effectively require that the equity be a publicly traded security. For a discussion of these concepts, the interested reader should consult any standard finance text.

Web Sites of Working Capital Market Participants

	2009 Revenues ($ millions)	Web Sites
Commercial Banks		
Bank of America Corp.	113,106.00	www.bankofamerica.com
Citigroup	112,372.00	www.citigroup.com
JPMorgan Chase and Co.	101,491.00	www.jpmorganchase.com
Wells Fargo	51,652.00	www.wellsfargo.com
U.S. Bancorp	19,229.00	www.usbank.com
Capital One Financial	17,868.50	www.capitalone.com
Bank of New York Mellon	16,355.00	www.bnymellon.com
State Street Corp.	12,922.00	www.statestreet.com
SunTrust Banks	12,800.80	www.suntrust.com
BB&T Corp.	10,404.00	www.bbt.com
Regions Financial	9,636.60	www.regions.com
Fifth Third Bancorp	8,554.00	www.53.com
PNC Financial Group	9,680.00	www.pnc.com
Key Bank	6,499.00	www.key.com
Northern Trust Corp.	5,677.90	www.northerntrust.com
Finance Companies		
GE Commercial Finance	27,228.90	www.ge.com
GMAC Commercial Finance		www.gmaccf.com

	2009 Revenues ($ millions)	Web Sites
1st Commercial Credit		www.1stcommercialcredit.com
ORIX Corporation	10,599.10	www.orix.com
CIT Group	6,228.90	www.cit.com
Textron Financial		www.textronfinancial.com
Other Vendors[*]		
ADP		www.adp.cpm
Administaff		www.administaff.com
Paychex		www.paychex.com
P & H Solutions		www.ph.com
Trinet Group		www.trinet.com
Troy Group (printing systems)		www.troygroup.com
Information Providers		
Barron's		www.barrons.com
Business Finance		www.businessfinance.com
Business Monitor International		www.businessmonitor.com
Business Week		www.businessweek.com
Dun and Bradstreet		www.dnb.com
The Economist		www.economist.com
Equifax		www.equifax.com
Euromoney		www.euromoney.com
Experian		www.experian.com
Forbes Magazine		www.forbes.com
Fortune Magazine		www.fortune.com
Handbook of Finance, 3 volumes, John Wiley & Sons, Inc. (F. Fabozzi, editor)		No website; library resource
Hoover's		www.hoovers.com
Journal of Corporate Accounting and Finance		www3.interscience.wiley.com/journal/60500170/home
Moody's		www.moodys.com

---

[*]For SCM vendors, see Exhibit 6.3.

	2009 Revenues ($ millions)	Web Sites
New York Times		www.nytimes.com
QFinance		www.qfinance.com
RMA		No website; library resource
Standard and Poor's		www.standardandpoors.com
Treasury and Risk Management		www.treasuryandrisk.com
Troy's Almanac		No website; library resource
Wall Street Journal		www.wsj.com
Government		
Federal Deposit Insurance Corporation		www.fdic.gov
Federal Reserve Bank		www.federalreserve.gov
Comptroller of the Currency		www.occ.treas.gov
Securities and Exchange Commission		www.sec.gov
Organizations		
American Institute of Certified Public Accountants		www.aicpa.com
American Bankers Association		www.aba.com
Association of Financial Professionals		www.afponline.org
Financial Executives International		www.fei.com
Phoenix Hecht		www.phoenixhecht.com

Glossary

The terms explained in this glossary are integral to the management of working capital. Acronyms and full word descriptions are included and are listed in order of general use (i.e., EOQ is listed first before economic order quantity, while application service provider is first listed before the acronym ASP). Other major terms are noted, but no attempt has been made to include every possible financial concept. Two excellent references on finance are *QFinance* and *Wiley Handbook of Finance*, listed in Appendix C.

A

Account analysis   A commercial bank's invoice for services provided to corporate customers. These statements are produced monthly, and contain such details as average daily book balance, average daily float, average available balances, itemized activity charges, earning credit rate, balances required to compensate for services, and balances available to support credit arrangements and other bank services.

Account maintenance   A basic charge for a bank account, to cover the overhead costs associated with the various services provided by the bank. Even if an account is idle, a maintenance charge is assessed. Typical charges are about $25 a month for middle market banks.

Account reconciliation   A bank service used to reconcile corporate bank accounts, providing a serial number listing of items paid (called *partial reconciliation*), or by matching a list of items issued (from a positive pay transmission) to the actual items paid, producing full reconcilement including outstanding items, balance by date, exceptions, and numerous optional reports.

Accounts payable A current liability that involves money owed to creditors representing obligations to pay for goods and services that have been purchased or acquired on credit terms.

Accounts receivable A current asset that represents amounts owed or the balance due to a vendor from a company for the goods sold or services rendered but not yet paid for.

Accrual accounting A method of keeping accounting records that attempts to match revenues and the accompanying costs incurred. A convention used in accrual accounting is depreciation, which expenses a capital good over its useful life.

ACH (Automated Clearing House) An organization that performs interbank clearing of paperless entries for participating financial institutions. ACHs are governed by operating rules and procedures developed by their participating financial institutions. ACHs make it possible for participating financial institutions to offer bill payment, direct payroll deposit, and other services.

Activity utilization Ratios that indicate how efficiently the business is using its assets. Important working capital utilization ratios are receivables turnover (and its complement, average collection period) and inventory turnover (and its complement, inventory turnover days).

Aging schedule An organization of accounts receivables classified by time intervals based on days due or past due; used to identify delinquency patterns.

Application service provider (ASP) A business that sells access to software applications through central servers over a communications network; this effectively outsources these information technology activities.

Asset-based finance (asset-based lending) A method of financing (lending) for rapidly growing and cash-strapped companies to meet their short-term cash needs; current assets (accounts receivable or inventory) are pledged as collateral.

Assets Any tangible or intangible valuable resource that a business entity owns, benefits from, or has use of in generating income and that could be converted to cash.

Available balances Those collected balances in an account that can be invested, disbursed, or wired out. Available balances are defined as book balances less float.

Availability The number of days that elapse between the deposit of checks and their accessibility for disbursement. An "availability schedule" lists drawee points or locations, specifying availability granted in business days. Availability is based on a bank's recent experience in clearing deposited checks.

B

Balance reporting Systems using a communications network to consolidate daily balance and activity information from one or more banks for the accounts of a specific user corporation. These systems consolidate information prior to opening of business and for report to the customer.

Banker's acceptance Endorsement of a draft or bill of exchange by the buyer's bank where the bank is obliged to pay the buyer's bill from a specified creditor when it is due on assurance of the buyer's financial strength and stability, and on payment of acceptance fee; primarily issued to finance international trade.

Bank information technology Internet-based systems that allow companies to electronically access a full range of financial services and execute many transactions; contains various modules accessible through a common interface.

Bank relationship management The process of managing the relationships between banks and companies in a comprehensive approach involving the credit and noncredit services offered by a bank and used by a company.

Bank statement A periodic statement of a customer's account detailing credits and debits posted to the account during the period and book balance as of the statement cutoff date.

Basel 2 A set of standards and regulations recommended by the Basel Committee on Bank Supervision that regulates banking and financing activities internationally; determines specific amounts of capital that financial institutions must hold to reduce the risks associated with lending and investing practices.

Basis point (BP) Market abbreviation for 1/100 of 1 percent, usually used in conjunction with comparisons of interest rates.

Beta The amount of systematic risk present in a particular asset relative to an average, usually defined as the Standard & Poor's 500 stock index. Systematic risk is a risk that affects a large number of assets (such as the financial system credit crisis of 2008–2009.)

Bill of lading A document issued by a carrier to a shipping company that specified goods have been received on board as cargo for transporting to a named place to a recipient (usually the purchaser).

Book balance The balance in a bank account that represents the net of debits and credits before any consideration for availability, reserve requirements, or other deductions.

C

Capital Asset Pricing Model (CAPM) A securities evaluation model that establishes the fair value of an investment by relating risk and expected return to the market as a whole; based on the theory that markets are efficient and prices of securities represent all known information about the security.

Capital budgeting   Refers to the analytical process of making long-term planning decisions by comparing the expected discounted cash flows with the internal rates of return (IRR) to determine the return from a capital investment; an alternative capital budgeting technique is net present value (NPV).

Cash accounting   In contrast to accrual accounting, cash accounting is a method where revenues are recorded when they are received and expenses when they are actually paid; no attempt is made to match revenues and costs incurred as in accrual accounting.

Cash budget   An estimate of cash receipts and disbursements for a future period, usually calculated daily by large companies and semi-weekly or weekly by middle market companies.

Cash discount   A reduction in the base price for the buyer by the seller where the buyer agrees to pay immediately or in a period shorter than the conventional period as set by the credit terms of sale; an example is 2/10, net 30, where the cash discount is 2 percent if the invoice is paid within 10 days of receipt with payment due in full within 30 days.

Cash letter   A batch of checks, accompanied by a letter detailing transit routings, amounts, and totals, sent directly to a bank or to another check clearing site, containing items drawn on that bank.

Check   A negotiable instrument or a written order instructing a bank to pay or draw against deposited funds for a specific amount of money to a designated person on demand by the person who draws the instrument.

Clearing (of checks)   A period of time between the deposit of a check by a payee to the receipt of the check by the drawee bank. Checks are cleared through the Federal Reserve System, clearing houses, and bank direct-send programs following presentation at the drawee bank.

Clearinghouse   A location where banks exchange and settle paper and electronic checks (i.e., ACHs) and where mutual claims are settled between the accounts of member depository institutions.

Commercial paper   A negotiable, discount note issued by investment grade issuers on an unsecured basis for up to a 9-month maturity. The yield on commercial paper normally exceeds the yield on U.S. Treasury Bills by 30 to 50 basis points given the additional risk of default.

Commodities futures   Contracts to buy or sell a commodity at a specific price on or before a certain date. Futures contracts are traded on organized exchanges (i.e., the Chicago Board of Trade) for a wide variety of agricultural, energy, foreign exchange, precious metal, interest rate, and other assets.

Common stock   A security that provides an investor with ownership and voting rights with limited liability; the owner is entitled to dividends (if declared) to share in a company's profits after taxes; these securities are often traded on organized stock exchanges (i.e., the New York Stock Exchange).

Comprehensive payables (or receivables)   The outsourcing of all or a major portion of a disbursement or collection activity. "Comprehensive payables" usually involves the company resolving all payment decisions and sending a transmission to a bank or vendor that processes the payment, including issuing checks or electronic payments and remittances advices, mailing payments, and reconciling clearing checks. "Comprehensive receivables" usually involves a bank or vendor receiving all remittances, depositing the items, and accounts receivable updating.

Concentration bank   Used as central point for all incoming or outgoing movement of funds from other corporate accounts. Generally this account is funded by deposits of incoming wire transfers, collection account transfers, and branch deposit concentrations. The account furnishes funds for outgoing wire transfers, disbursing account transfers, and charges for ACH.

Controlled disbursement   A checking account service capable of providing a total of the checks that will be charged to the customer's account(s) early each business day.

Corporate governance   Administration of a business through rules, processes, or laws regarding responsible behavior as referenced by the ownership, management, employees, customers, and other stakeholders; required of public companies operating in the United States as mandated in the Sarbanes–Oxley Act of 2002.

Cost of capital or weighted average cost of capital (WACC)   The weighted average of a firm's cost of debt (after tax) and cost of equity (common stock and retained earnings). The WACC is expressed as a percentage.

Cost of goods sold   An income statement account that includes all the expenses associated with the manufacturing costs of a company's products including its raw materials, work in process, finished goods, and shipping expenses.

Counterparty   An entity with whom one negotiates for a particular transaction, with the counterparty on the opposite side of the transaction.

Country risk assessment (CRA)   The quantification of the possibility that transactions with international counterparties may be interrupted by the interference of the foreign government or due to local conditions; measured through the analysis of political and economic risks.

Credit reporting   Procedures that review the credit history of a company or a person using detailed information on credit accounts and loans, payment history, and other recent financial data.

Current assets   The total of cash and other assets that are readily converted to cash within one year, helping to satisfy liquidity needs for daily operations. Assets with a life of greater than one year are *fixed assets*.

Current liabilities   The funds owed by a company that are to be settled or paid off within a year.

Current ratio   A financial ratio that measures the capability of the firm to pay its debt over the next year; defined as current assets divided by current liabilities.

D

Days' sales outstanding (DSO)   A company's average collection
   period in days. The calculation is 360 days divided by receivables turnover. Receivables turnover is credit sales divided by accounts receivable.

Debit   An accounting entry on the left side in a double-entry accounting system. The parallel right-side entry is called a *credit*.

Debt collection agency   An independent business that pursues payments on unpaid debts owed by individuals or businesses, usually for
   balances older than 90 days past due.

Demand deposit   Deposited funds that are available to the customer
   at any time during regular business hours, and that require no advance notice of withdrawal. They are usually accessed by writing a
   check. Checking accounts are the most common form of demand
   deposit. The required reserve against time deposits is 10 percent.

Deposit reporting service (DRS)   A service that mobilizes funds in
   local depository accounts to the concentration account.

Depreciation   A convention used in accrual accounting that attempts
   to match the expense of a fixed asset for a specific reporting period
   with the revenue it produces.

Direct deposit   An ACH service that permits a company to pay its
   employees without writing checks. The company generates credit
   entries representing deposits and delivers them to its financial institution before each payday, which posts them to employee bank
   accounts on payday.

Discount rate   The rate of interest charged by the Federal Reserve on
   loans it makes to member banks. This rate influences the rates banks
   charge their customers.

Distribution method   A forecasting technique that estimates the distribution of cash flow by day of the week and day of the month.

Dividend yield   A percentage indicating the amount a company pays
   out as a dividend each year; measured by dividing the annual dividend payment by the stock price.

Drawee bank The bank on which an item is drawn and to which it must be presented to collect cash.

Dynamic discounting The situation when vendors offer prorated cash discounts based on days paid prior to the due date.

E

Earnings credit rate (ECR) A rate used by a bank to determine the earnings allowance associated with a customer's demand deposit balances. Depending upon the bank, the rate may be arbitrarily set or tied to some market rate, such as Federal funds.

Electronic commerce (E-commerce or EC) The exchange of business information in an electronic format in an agreed-upon standard.

Encoding An amount that is magnetic ink character recognition (MICR) encoded in the lower right corner with the check amount, using special MICR printing equipment.

Enterprise resource planning (ERP) system An integrated system that manages internal and external company resources including tangible assets, financial resources, and materials purchasing. ERP systems are based on a centralized computing platform, consolidating all significant business operations into a uniform environment.

EOQ (economic order quantity) The optimal quantity to order from a supplier that minimizes the total costs of processing orders and the cost of holding inventory.

Equity A stock or any security that represents ownership interest in a corporation.

F

Factoring The sale or transfer of title of a company's accounts receivable to a third party, the factor.

Fed funds (Federal funds) Reserves traded among banks for overnight investment and to fund a bank's deficit position with the

Federal Reserve System. Most U.S. interest rate transactions (such as bank credit arrangements) are quoted as an increment from Federal funds.

Fedwire (Federal wire transfer) The Federal Reserve System's electronic communications network used in transferring member bank reserve account balances and government securities as well as other related information. This network interconnects the Federal Reserve offices, the Treasury, various government agencies, and the member banks.

Financial leverage The degree to which borrowed money is utilized to increase volume in production, sales, and earnings; generally, the higher the amount of debt, the greater the financial leverage.

Fiscal year The accounting period chosen by a company for its reporting period. Any year end may be chosen by management, although companies usually choose a quiet period when sales activity is at a seasonal low.

Fixed assets Long-term assets with lives greater than one year that cannot be easily converted into cash, including manufacturing equipment, furniture, office equipment, or any other tangible assets held for business use; contrast fixed assets to current assets.

Float Refers to the status of funds in the process of collection or disbursement. Float has the dimensions of money and interest and thus is computed as the product of funds being collected or disbursed and the applicable interest rate. This product is expressed in dollars (or other currency).

Foreign exchange (FX) The buying and selling of currencies worldwide, consists of the currencies themselves, the transfer mechanisms, and the information needed to make sound multicurrency decisions. FX services are needed when more than one currency is involved in an international business transaction. Most of the EU transacts its business in the euro (€), which replaced national currencies (except for the British pound [£], the Danish krone, and the Swedish krona).

Forward foreign exchange rates   Hedging the delivery of a foreign currency on a specified later date by arranging with a bank to "lock in" a guaranteed rate when it is likely that an international transaction will settle at a future time.

G

Gross profit (or gross margin)   The income statement account that is calculated by subtracting the cost of goods sold from sales (revenues).

Growth yield (capital gain)   The component of a business's cost of equity capital that calculates investor expectations for an increase in the stock price, usually measured for the period of one year. The other component of the cost of equity capital is the dividend yield.

H

Hedge   A transaction that mitigates exposure to a risk by taking a position opposite to the initial position; hedging instruments include forwards, options, swaps, and futures contracts.

I

Imaging   The capture of an electronic picture of the check and/or remittance document received, which can be archived, retrieved, and transmitted to the company.

Interest yield   The expected return on a debt security measured by dividing the interest paid for one year by the price of the debt security. Except for tax-free municipal bonds, the final cost to a business is then reduced by the appropriate tax deduction (calculated as 1 − the tax rate).

Intrabank transfer   A transfer of funds within a bank between accounts; an example is the funding of a bank's controlled disbursement account from a concentration account in that bank.

Inventory financing   Asset-based financing used to gain working capital, with a company's inventory functioning as the collateral for the loan.

Inventory turnover   A ratio calculated as cost of goods sold divided by inventory, showing the utilization of that asset as compared to a peer group of companies.

IRR (internal rate of return)   A capital budgeting procedure; it is the discount rate that forces the net present value of a proposed capital investment equal to zero.

J

Just-in-time (JIT)   A method of managing inventory levels to minimize working capital. Successful implementation depends on strict production planning/control techniques and integrated communications with suppliers and customers.

L

Letter of credit (LC)   An instrument primarily used in international business transactions; issued by a bank to an individual or corporation that allows the bank to substitute its own credit for that of the individual or corporation.

Liabilities   A major portion of a balance sheet showing amounts owed to vendors and lenders. The current portion shows amount due to be paid within one year; the long-term portion shows the amounts due beyond one year.

LIBOR   The London Interbank Offering Rate on funds traded between banks. Some interest rate transactions (such as bank credit arrangements) are quoted as an increment from LIBOR, although most transactions in the United States are based on Federal funds.

Liquidity   The cash used in a normal business environment, including operating cash flow, short-term investments, and credit sources.

Line of credit (credit line)   A prearranged amount of credit a lender will extend to a company over a specified period of time, usually one year.

Loan covenants   Restrictions established by lenders on borrowers that apply to lines of credit and other types of credit agreements, requiring a certain level of performance.

Lockboxing   A collection mechanism in which mail containing payments bypasses corporate offices, going directly to a post office box maintained by the bank of deposit, thereby reducing collection float. After deposit of the check, remittance advices, photocopies of the check, and other supporting material are forwarded to the corporate credit department. Wholesale processing provides check copies and original remittance documents to the client; retail processing captures encoded MICR and/or OCR information on the bottom of the check and/or remittance documents and transmits it to the client in a data file.

Long-term liabilities   See "liabilities"; includes loans (e.g., mortgages payable) and bonds payable.

M

MICR (also OCR)   Acronyms for magnetic ink character recognition and optical character recognition; a set of unique characters printed on a check or remittance advice that are scannable by reader–sorter equipment.

Money market mutual funds (MMMFs)   Pools of various types of short-term investments that offer shares to corporate (and individual) investors through the format of mutual funds.

Multicurrency account   A single international bank account with the capability to receive deposits and withdrawals of major currencies; used to simplify the management of foreign exchange.

Munis (municipal securities)   State and local government municipal securities that have their interest payment exempt from federal taxes; yields are less than those of other investment instruments.

N

NACHA   The electronic payments association that establishes rules for ACH transactions.

Netting   A system used to reduce the number of counterparty payments by summing debits and credits and transferring the resulting balance. Netting systems are used in cross-border payments and in industries where there are many individual transactions, such as in broker–dealer activities.

Net worth   The accounting determination of a company's value based on its total assets less total liabilities.

NPV (net present value)   A capital budgeting technique that calculates the difference between the cost of an investment and the present value of all predictable future cash inflows. Also see IRR.

NSF (not sufficient funds)   The situation when a check is presented for clearing and sufficient funds are not in the maker's bank account. The bank may reject (bounce) the check unless the maker has arranged overdraft protection.

O

Outsourcing   Bank or vendor processing of a business activity not considered as core or critical to profitability. Examples include cash handling activities, certain information processing, and other functions.

Owner's equity   A balance-sheet account that shows the amount of a business that has been paid in by the shareholders for their stock; the other major category in net worth is retained earnings.

P

Payback method   A capital budgeting procedure that calculates the time required by an investment to generate sufficient cash flow to recover the initial cost.

Paycard   ATM cards specifically issued for payroll. An employee receiving a paycard need not have an account at the payroll bank.

Instead, the card is issued along with a PIN number, allowing access through any ATM machine or at merchants that accept the card family (e.g., Visa or MasterCard).

PO (purchase order) A commercial document indicating types, quantities, and prices for products or services the seller will provide to the buyer. Sending a PO to a supplier constitutes a legal offer to buy products or services. Acceptance of a PO by a seller usually forms a contract between the buyer and seller.

Pooling A product offered by international financial institutions that aggregates the debit and credit balances of a company's separate bank accounts to calculate a net balance, with interest paid or charged on the net debit or credit.

Positive pay A bank service used to reduce disbursement fraud, with the issuer sending an issued file to its bank of serial numbers and check amounts. Only those checks that match this listing are paid.

Preferred stock Ownership shares in a business with dividend priority over common stock, normally with a fixed dividend rate, sometimes without voting rights.

Presentment The actual delivery of a negotiable instrument by a holder to the drawee bank for payment or acceptance.

Presort (for postage discount) A discount to regular first-class postage provided by the USPS based on a minimum quantity of letters presorted by zip code.

Procurement (purchasing) cards A payment mechanism involving the use of credit cards by authorized company employees for routine purchases.

Profitability A measure of a business's net income after taxes, either as a sheer calculation or compared to owners' equity or sales.

Pro forma statement A financial statement prepared on the basis of assumptions of future events that affect the expected condition of the company driven by those events or actions. For example, assumptions as to future sales levels generally enable a company to project anticipated income.

Q

Quick ratio   A liquidity ratio with current assets less inventory in the numerator and current liabilities in the denominator.

R

Ratio analysis   A financial technique that allows the examination of a company's financial statements. It compares a numerator and a denominator to changes over time and/or against its competitors.

Receivables turnover   A calculation of receivables efficiency, calculated as credit sales divided by accounts receivable.

Reinvoicing center   A central financial subsidiary used by a multinational company to reduce transaction exposure by billing all home country exports in the home currency and reinvoicing to each operating affiliate in that affiliate's local currency.

Remittance advice   Information on a document attached to the check (such as an invoice) by the drawer, which tells the payee why a payment is being made.

Repo (repurchase agreement)   A holder of securities sells securities (usually U.S. Treasuries) to an investor with an agreement to repurchase them at a fixed price on a fixed date, usually overnight. The security "buyer" effectively lends the "seller" money for the period of the agreement.

Reserve requirement   A portion of financial institution deposits that must be kept on deposit by member banks at the Federal Reserve.

Retained earnings   The accumulation on a company's balance sheet of net profits after taxes not paid out in dividends.

Revolving term loan   Loans for periods longer than one year (sometimes called "revolvers") and lasting for up to five years.

RFP (request for proposal) A formal document soliciting responses to specific questions in several areas. The typical RFP begins with a description of the organization, including its locations, the number of transactions, banks and vendors currently used, and other pertinent data. A statement is provided regarding the specific requirements to be addressed by the proposal, including the timing of the selection process and of implementation.

Risk The possibility of loss or injury. The measurement of risk has traditionally been through the frequency of human or property loss in specific categories, such as death or disability by age, sex, and occupation or the frequency of fire damage to specific types of construction at various locations. Newer techniques have been used to manage business risk.

Risk-free return The return from an investment without risk, usually defined as the rate on U.S. Treasury bills. This rate reflects the absence of default risk and inflation risk.

Risk management The attempt to identify, prioritize, and quantify the risks from sources that threaten the working capital and strategic objectives of the corporation. This effort can be directed to individual risks or to risks that transcend company operations.

Risk premium The excess return required from an investment in a risky asset over that required from a risk-free investment. Used in the calculation of the CAPM.

S

Sales financing Lending money for the purpose of selling capital goods through a contractual installment sales agreement. Companies provide loans to businesses where the collateral of the loan is the goods purchased.

SCM (supply chain management) An integrated system to optimize all of the components of a manufacturing process, including purchasing, inventory management, and transportation logistics. Two key concepts in SCM are EOQ and JIT.

Securitization   A financing technique in which a company issues securities backed by packages of assets with regular income flows, such as mortgages or car payments.

Spot foreign exchange rates   The standard format for commercial foreign exchange transactions, with delivery in two business days.

Sweep   A bank account from which all the funds above a specified figure are automatically transferred out of the account for investment overnight, and then returned to the bank account next day.

T

Tax advantaged centers   A service offered in several countries offering low corporate taxes and other benefits to attract multinational companies; the host country anticipates that corporations will establish offices for the management of their various business functions. In return, the local economy receives economic activity and employment.

Time deposit   An interest-bearing deposit at a banking institution, either with a specified maturity (a "certificate of deposit" or CD) or open-ended (a "savings account"). Time deposits by regulation require notification to the institution for redemption, although in practice they will honor requests for savings accounts distributions on demand.

Time value of money   The calculation of the present value of a future sum, or the future value of a present sum.

Times interest earned   A ratio that measures the amount of interest paid against earnings before interest and taxes, or EBIT divided by interest expense.

Transaction exposure   A risk that results from the movement in foreign exchange rates between the time a transaction is booked and the time it settles.

Transit routing number (TRN or ABA [American Banking Association] number) A series of machine-readable digits on a check that facilitate the routing for collection of funds from the drawee bank by the Federal Reserve. The TRN appears in the MICR line at the bottom of the instrument as well as in the fraction in the upper right hand corner. The number represents the Federal Reserve District of the drawee bank, the Federal Reserve Bank head office or branch through which the item should be cleared, and the bank-specific address. A ninth digit may be present, which is a verification of the logic of the TRN.

Translation exposure The balance-sheet exposure that results when a company consolidates its financial statements and is required to report the change in the net value of its foreign currency assets. The exposure results from fluctuations in FX that change the rate at which the net assets are valued.

U

Uniform Commercial Code (UCC) A set of regulations covering commercial transactions adopted by the individual states. The UCC defines the rights and duties of the parties in commercial transactions and provides a statutory definition of commonly used business practices.

V

Value at Risk (VaR) An approach to determining the risk exposure in a portfolio of assets. Although certain risks (e.g., financial instruments, credit, commodity prices) can be forced into the VaR model, it is a process that is heavily dependent on historical patterns.

Value dating The determination of a future date on which payment will be credited in a bank; used in some countries instead of availability (but not in the United States).

W

WIP (work in process)   A category of inventory that represents materials that are in the process of being manufactured into saleable finished goods.

Working capital   The difference between a firm's current assets and current liabilities, measured in dollars or another currency. Working capital is also the amount of money available for use in operating the business.

U.S. Legislation Significant to Working Capital Management

Federal Reserve Act of 1913   Widespread bank failures and panics continued from the end of the Civil War until the Panic of 1907. As the result, Congress adopted the Federal Reserve Act in 1913. The Act established the Federal Reserve System as the central bank of the United States. The purpose was to provide a stable currency, to improve supervision of banking and to stabilize interest rates and the money supply.

McFadden Act of 1927   Restricted commercial banks to doing business within the state in which they were chartered (with certain exceptions).

Glass–Steagall Act of 1933   Separated commercial and investment banking activities, forcing such firms as J.P. Morgan to split (into Morgan Guaranty Bank and Morgan Stanley). Congress believed that such a separation was necessary to prevent the types of transactions that may have caused the stock market crash in October 1929.

Riegle–Neal Act of 1994   Deregulated banks, permitting mergers across state lines provided they were adequately capitalized and managed. Prior to Riegle-Neal, banks were limited to doing business within the states in which they were chartered, as mandated by the McFadden Act of 1927.

Gramm-Leach-Bliley Act of 1999   Created the concept of the financial holding company, authorizing these organizations to engage in underwriting and selling insurance and securities, conduct both commercial and merchant banking, and invest in and develop real estate and other activities. The Act repealed the Glass-Steagall Act (see above).

Sarbanes-Oxley Act of 2002   Enacted as a reaction to a number of major corporate and accounting scandals. These losses cost investors billions of dollars when the share prices of affected companies collapsed, shaking public confidence in the securities markets. Two important sections of Sarbanes-Oxley dealt with corporate responsibility and enhanced financial disclosures.

Check Clearing for the 21st Century Act of 2004 (Check 21)   Allowed the electronic delivery of check images, significantly speeding the processing. It allows the recipient of an original check to create a digital version and eliminates the need for further handling of the physical document.

Financial Reform Act of 2010   Ended the possibility that taxpayers will be asked to bail out financial firms that threaten the economy (known as "too big to fail"). This was accomplished by creating a process to liquidate failed financial firms; imposing tough new capital and leverage requirements that make it undesirable to grow too large; updating the authority of the Federal Reserve to allow system-wide support, but no longer subsidize individual firms; and establishing rigorous standards and supervision.

About the Author

Dr. James S. Sagner is with the School of Business of the University of Bridgeport (CT) teaching MBA-level courses in finance and international business, and is senior principal of Sagner/Marks. He has managed over 250 large-scale studies for global organizations and is recognized as an expert in financial management and economic analysis. His clients have included financial service and manufacturing companies. Previously, he was with the First National Bank of Chicago (now JPMorgan Chase); A. T. Kearney, financial and economic consultants; and served as Chief Economist of the Maryland Department of Transportation.

He is the author of 7 books and over 60 papers and articles that have appeared in various publications. In addition, he teaches in the executive education program at the University of North Carolina. Dr. Sagner received his BS from Washington and Lee University, his MBA from the Wharton School of the University of Pennsylvania, and his PhD in Business and Economics from The American University. Sagner, who was honored as a Rockefeller Fellow, is a CCM, CMC, and a member of Beta Gamma Sigma.

Index

Printed in the United States
By Bookmasters